THE RUGBY LEAGUE MYTH

The Forgotten Clubs of Lancashire, Cheshire and Furness

by
Michael Latham
Tom Mather

First published September 1993 in Great Britain
by
Mike RL Publications
28 Windermere Drive
Adlington PR6 9PD

All rights reserved. No part of this publication may be reproduced, stored in a retrieval system, or transmitted in any form or by any means, electronic, mechanical, photocopying, recording or otherwise without the prior permission in writing of the Copyright holders, nor be otherwise circulated in any form or binding or cover other than in which it is published and without a similar condition including this condition being imposed on the subsequent publisher.

© copyright Mike RL Publications, 1993

ISBN 0 9516098 3 1

Designed, typeset and produced by Coveropen Ltd., Wigan.

Set via high resolution DTP in 9/10.5pt Flange light.

Printed and bound in Great Britain.

CONTENTS

1	The Myth Explored	7
2	The Battle for Survival	14
3	The Lancashire Second Competition	19
4	Altrincham	21
5	Barrow	25
6	Barton	30
7	Birkenhead Wanderers	34
8	Blackpool	41
9	Crompton	45
10	Dalton	49
11	Fleetwood	52
12	Lancaster	57
13	Leigh Shamrocks	62
14	Millom	66
15	Morecambe	70
16	Radcliffe	76
17	St Helens Recs	82
18	Tyldesley	87
19	Ulverston	92
20	Walkden	97
21	Werneth	102
22	Whitworth	105

Michael Latham (32) was born in Leigh and brought up in Bolton. He graduated in 1982 with an honours degree in Economic and Social History from Bristol University. He is now an accountant by profession.

He has been a lifelong supporter of Leigh RLFC and Bolton Wanderers.

An active member of the RL Record Keepers' Club, he is a regular contributor to club programmes, newspapers and periodicals and devotes much of his spare time to researching the game's history and statistics. This is his fourth book.

Married to Janet with two young children Jennifer and Sarah, he lives in Adlington, near Chorley.

Tom Mather was born in 1947 at Lower Ince, near Wigan. After attending Spring View School (as had Roy Evans the former Wigan and GB loose forward), he began his working life at Hawker Siddeley in the aircraft industry.

On completion of his apprenticeship, he moved to Winnipeg, Canada, returning two years later to enter teacher training college. As a teacher he moved to the Fylde Coast and has lived there since 1973.

His first writing experience came with his work on the *History of Fleetwood Northern Union Club*. This first brought him into contact with Michael Latham and has resulted in this book. He periodically writes articles for the *Rugby Leaguer* newspaper.

Married, with two children, he enjoys watching rugby-being too old to play it. He also enjoys researching that era of rugby known as the "breakaway".

He is now head of Psychology at Lytham High School.

INTRODUCTION AND ACKNOWLEDGEMENTS

WHEN we first had the idea to write this book, it was not our intention to be controversial. We intended, simply, to produce a book which would extend the existing knowledge of rugby in Lancashire, Cheshire and Furness and in particular to publicise the many long-forgotten clubs which made such a contribution to the events leading up to and following the breakaway in 1895. We decided to concentrate on the clubs which made up the Lancashire Second Competition during its brief existence from 1897 to 1901.

In the beginning we were believers in the traditional and accepted view of the events leading to the formation of the Northern Union. However, when we began to research those clubs which were not in the "hotbed" of rugby, but rather on the fringes, a different view began to emerge.

It was a view which, to substantiate, required a vast amount of detective work in libraries across Lancashire, Cheshire and Cumbria. The results of our efforts are produced in these pages and present an alternative viewpoint of the breakaway. Like all historians, we are, after all this time, dependent upon the printed word, which is always likely to reflect the sometimes biased views of the writer or be misinterpreted by the present day reader.

However, it is our belief that the newspaper reporters of the time, because of the status and location of the clubs they wrote about, did so with perhaps a more dispassionate view than did their colleagues situated in the heartlands of Lancashire and Yorkshire. The book will, we hope, present an insight into a fascinating period in the history of the game.

During the course of our research we were indebted to the help and expertise provided by staff at the following libraries: Altrincham, Bacup, Barrow, Birkenhead, Blackpool, Bolton, Bury, Chorley, Fleetwood, Lancaster, Leigh, Morecambe, Oldham, Preston, Radcliffe, Salford, St Helens, Walkden and Wigan.

Files and microfilms from the following newspapers were studied: *Altrincham & Bowdon Guardian, Barrow News, Birkenhead News, Birkenhead Visitor, Bolton Evening News, Bury Times, Eccles Journal, Farnworth & Worsley Journal, Fleetwood Chronicle, Fleetwood Express, The Football Field, Lancashire Daily Post, Lancaster Guardian, Leigh Chronicle, Leigh Journal, Morecambe Visitor, North Western Daily Mail, Oldham Chronicle, Radcliffe Times, Rochdale Observer, Salford Reporter, St Helens Newspaper and Advertiser, St Helens Reporter, Ulverston Advertiser, Wigan Examiner* and *Wigan Observer.*

Special thanks are due to Bob Rushton for the cover design/artwork and to our wives, for putting up with the whole business.

Others who have supplied invaluable assistance in the form of illustrations or the supply and verification of facts have been Robert Gate, Timothy Auty, Nigel Winnard, Irene Winnard, Ian Jackson, Robin Isherwood, Graham Morris, Trevor Delaney, John Edwards, Jim Broadbent, Bill Dalton, Terry Alexander, Alf Yates, Mike Hulme, Jim Heyes, Whitworth Museum, Joe Griffiths, Mrs Bill Curtis, Mrs CE Mullineux, Irvin Saxton and the RL Record Keepers' Club, Cheshire County Archives and Local Studies and The Rugby Football League.

Books specifically referred to include:
Keith Nutter & Don Pettingale, The History of Barrow (1981)
Trevor Delaney, The Roots of Rugby League (1984)
Nigel Winnard, A History of Chorley Rugby Club (unpublished 1993)
Athletic News Football Annuals 1886-87 to 1900-01, facsimilies published by the Association of Football Statisticians (1986)
Niel Wood, Pilkington Recreation RLFC (Code 13 issue 2, December 1986)
   Ordnance Survey kindly gave permission to reproduce Ordnance Survey extracts.
   We would also like to thank the *Rugby Leaguer* and *League Express* newspapers for publicising the book and extend our gratitude to all the people who took out an advance subscription. Without the support of subscribers this book would never have seen the light of day.
   Finally, we hope the reader will get as much pleasure from reading the book as we did in researching and writing it.

Michael Latham
Tom Mather
August 1993

PUBLISHER'S APOLOGY
The publisher wishes to apologise for the inferior quality of many photographs. This is entirely due to the inferior quality of the originals due to age. On balance, it was decided that the majority of readers would prefer their inclusion.

The Myth Explored

THE old Queen continued her reign as if immortal. The red of the British Empire dominated the world map. Few could remember otherwise. 1895 saw Oscar Wilde acclaimed for "The Importance of Being Earnest" before other matters put him in prison. Kipling completed his second "Jungle Book"; even Gilbert and Sullivan were persuaded to sink their differences and resume collaboration.

Sunderland won the Football League and Aston Villa the FA Cup with England trouncing Scotland 3-0. The summer brought Surrey the newly constituted County Championship closely followed by Lancashire for whom Archie MacLaren scored a record 424 runs at Taunton. Superficially, all was well in Victorian Britain.

The General Election gave the Unionist Party (Conservative) a large majority but only one in seven of the population had the vote and the North was largely disenfranchised. The steady march of Trade Unionism continued inexorably. The six day working week was the norm. Thus, a man playing rugby on a Saturday afternoon lost wages which he could ill-afford. Were the match away from home, the greater the loss. This was recognised in the North of England by what were known as broken-time payments. Gate-taking clubs could easily circumvent the amateur regulations and the local Unions, particularly in Lancashire, tended to turn a blind eye. This thinly disguised practice has hitherto been regarded as the main reason for the myth developing.

In 1888 Shaw and Shrewsbury, two professional cricketers, organised the first rugby trip to Australia by an English side. The 21 players (14 from Lancashire and Yorkshire clubs) were away from March to November 1888. On their return, the Rugby Union required them to sign affidavits as to their amateur status. One would be naive in the extreme to believe that it would be possible for them to travel half way round the world to play rugby without financial assistance.

The Maori visit of 1888-89 attracted huge crowds, playing a marathon 74 matches in 25 weeks. They demanded two-thirds of the gate money as their guarantee. Could they possibly have returned to New Zealand unblemished?

Though broken-time payments were tacitly accepted, problems arose when the richer clubs began offering inducements to players from other clubs to transfer their allegiance or when an outstanding footballer from afar was found a convenient job in the locality.

From the Yorkshire committee, the Rev Frank Marshall, zealot of amateurism, took upon himself the role of inquisitor as he attempted to uncover breaches of the regulations. Though he met with a marked lack of cooperation, suspensions did result. Across the Pennines there was no need for a Marshall as the clubs began accusing each other of poaching players and making illegal payments. Again, several clubs were suspended.

Yorkshire had long been jealous of the Southern dominance of the Rugby Union. Efforts to share the AGM alternately between London and the North had failed. Yorkshire provided the Rugby Union with over 40% of its clubs and in playing terms was easily the strongest county.

In London on 20 September 1893, the Yorkshire representatives, Miller and Newsome, proposed that "players be allowed compensation for bona-fide loss of time." A counter motion put forward by Union Secretary Rowland Hill was passed by 282-136. 120 proxy votes, many of dubious authenticity, bolstered the winners.

William Cail was set the task of drawing up anti-professional legislation.

Two years later, on 29 August 1895, twenty-two Rugby Union clubs from Lancashire, Yorkshire and Cheshire formed a Northern Rugby Football Union (retitled the Rugby Football League in 1922).

The traditional view is that the Northern Union was formed due to disagreements over the issue of broken-time. The aim of this study is to present additional material, from the stance of those in the slipstream of the senior clubs, which lends weight to an alternative viewpoint.

Attention is focussed on the nineteen clubs which, from 1897 to 1901, competed in the Lancashire Second Competition. Of those, only one, Barrow, was still functioning as a professional club by 1907, hardly the picture of a healthy, growing organisation. Many of the clubs had fine traditions in the Rugby Union game, enjoyed strong local support and were the focal point for sport in their community. A few years later many had gone to the wall and professional rugby, in most cases, never returned.

New clubs, Fleetwood and Blackpool, formed specifically to play the Northern Union game, struggled from the outset, with precious little support from the governing body. Others, in the shadow of a long-established senior club, such as Crompton, Werneth and Whitworth, simply could not compete and disbanded. Yet, within the Rugby Union, the senior and junior clubs had co-existed, if not in perfect harmony, at least in a reasonably co-operative manner.

Some clubs, by their geographical location on the fringes of the action, Ulverston, Millom, Dalton, Birkenhead and Altrincham saw their best players lured away and found the expenses of competing in the Northern Union simply too prohibitive.

Barton, a junior club, tried to speculate to accumulate, but found itself enveloped under mounting debts. Radcliffe, Walkden and St Helens Recs found themselves in competition with the fast-growing game of association football which, by contrast, was able to expand whilst nurturing its junior clubs more successfully.

The seeds of the Northern Union were sown much earlier. The clubs needed guaranteed fixtures, playing in a competitive league, which would attract large crowds. The idea of a league was not a new one by any means but such ambitions were strongly frowned upon by the Rugby Union whose official view was that such a move would result in a further step down the road to professionalism.

The precedent had already been established in association football when the Football League was founded in 1888. Of the twelve founder members, six were from Lancashire, Preston North End, Bolton Wanderers, Accrington, Burnley, Blackburn Rovers and Everton and the other half, broadly speaking, from the Midlands, Aston Villa, West Bromwich Albion, Wolverhampton Wanderers, Stoke, Derby County and Notts County. The South was not represented for the simple reason that there was no professional football club below Birmingham. Yorkshire was dominated by the oval ball game, though soccer was beginning to make inroads.

Three years earlier, in 1885, the Football League clubs had presented themselves as "professionals" to the Football Association. The Football Association accepted them as such and the game progressed. The rugby game in the North mirrored these happenings of a decade previously but the Rugby Union lacked the vision of the Football Association. History was not about to repeat itself.

Mindful of the need to fight the challenge from soccer, fast growing in popularity, rugby clubs in West Lancashire formed their own union in November 1884. Twenty-four clubs competed in the first West Lancashire Cup in the 1885-86 season and some large crowds were attracted, the highest 15000 for a cup tie between Warrington and Runcorn at Widnes.

By September 1886, fifty clubs were in membership and a Junior Challenge Cup was

THE NORTHERN UNION IN THE NORTH WEST FROM 1895

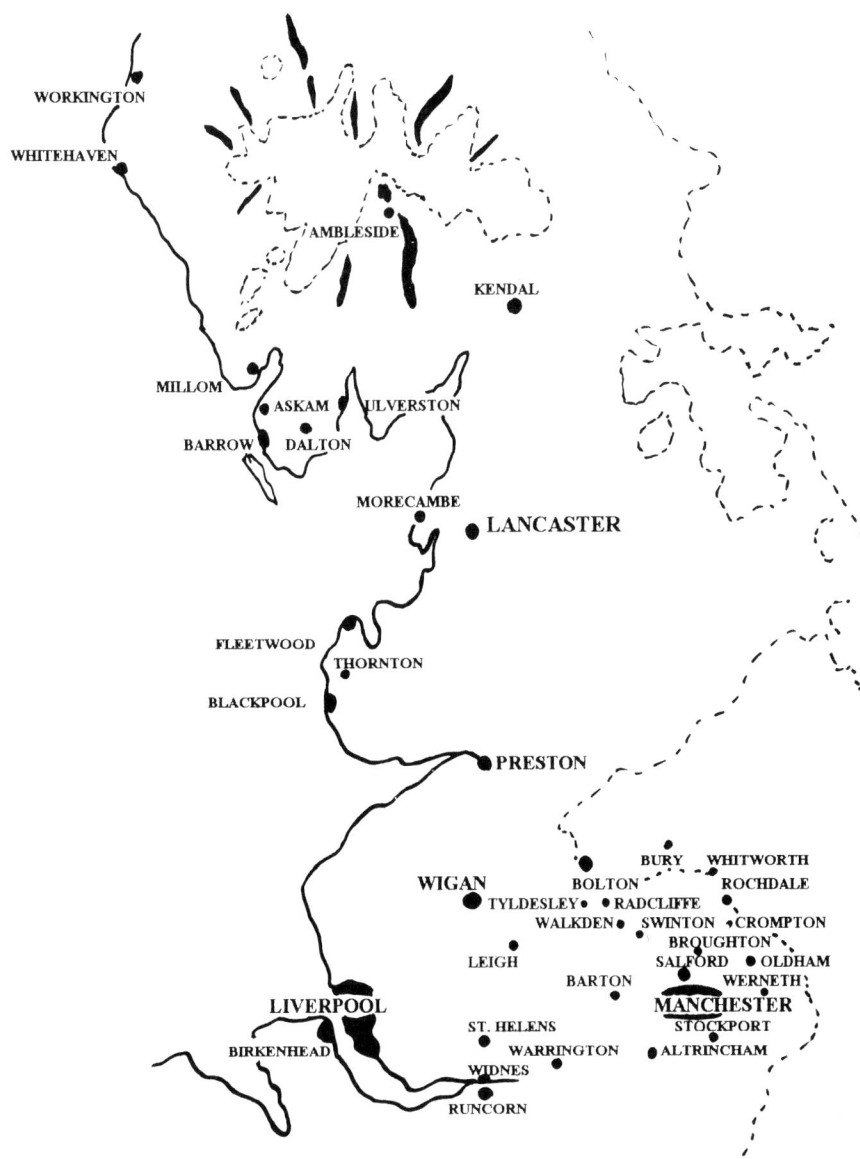

promoted. At the Annual Meeting on 31 May 1889, it was decided to form a league competition to replace the knock-out system. "Now all the excitement will be spread across the whole season instead of being compressed into one month" reported the *Wigan Examiner*. Eight clubs were elected to the league, Aspull, Warrington, Wigan, Tyldesley, Leigh, Walkden, St Helens and Widnes.

On the face of it, the league proved a great innovation but problems arose as clubs objected to some of the rulings of the committee. It lasted only two seasons but the West Lancashire League was the shape of things to come.

The Yorkshire Cup was first contested in 1877 and had been a tremendous success. At the end of the 1891-92 season twelve senior Yorkshire clubs, Batley, Bradford, Brighouse Rangers, Dewsbury, Halifax, Huddersfield, Hull, Hunslet, Leeds, Liversedge, Manningham and Wakefield Trinity took one step further and formed an Alliance. They wished to form a league which they, rather than the Yorkshire County, would control and organise. Not surprisingly the Yorkshire Union did not take kindly to the idea of relinquishing its authority and so refused to sanction the proposed moves.

The Yorkshire Union eventually set up a sub-committee, made up of one member from each of the Alliance clubs. Old Ebor, writing in *The Athletic News Football Annual* of 1892-93, wrote "The result of the hubbub is that the Alliance is dead and buried, but in its place we have the official Yorkshire Football Rugby Union Senior Competition".

So was the Yorkshire first division born and with it the power of the clubs enhanced.

Across the Pennines, the Lancashire clubs were also organising themselves. The result was the establishment of the Lancashire Club Championship in October 1892 involving ten clubs, Broughton, Broughton Rangers, Oldham, Rochdale Hornets, St Helens Recs, Salford, Swinton, Tyldesley, Warrington and Wigan.

The uneasy relationship between the Lancashire and Yorkshire Unions and the first division clubs reached breaking point at the end of the 1894-95 season, particularly in Yorkshire. Clubs in the lower divisions had been pressing for the right of automatic promotion to the first division which was denied them, though test matches for promotion did take place in Lancashire.

Matters came to a head when the two bottom clubs in the Senior Competition, Hull and Wakefield Trinity, were re-elected at the expense of the champions and runners-up in the Second Competition, Morley and Castleford. The senior clubs clearly considered that the re-elected clubs would provide better gates than those seeking to replace them. Financial considerations outweighed the idea of promotion on merit.

Old Ebor reflected in *The Athletic News Football Annual* of 1895-96 "The Senior Competition, for which the leading clubs so tenaciously and successfully fought three years ago, has ceased to exist....Unfortunately, the broader view was not taken; the two lowest clubs in the Senior Competition were re-elected and no explanation of the reasons for this course of action and no statement as to the committee's intentions regarding the future were furnished."

The Yorkshire Union used its right of veto against the Senior Competition. As Old Ebor wrote "They (the Union Committee) therefore vetoed the Senior Competition. The latter simply accepted the veto and resigned from the Yorkshire Union, still without a word of explanation of their policy."

In Lancashire the senior clubs were determined to have the same power as their counterparts. *The Lancashire Daily Post* of Monday 6 May 1895 reported "The clubs comprising the first class championship competition have got angry with the Lancashire Rugby Union. The clubs have demanded that the competition shall be placed in their hands and this has been refused. In consequence the meeting for arrangement of fixtures which ought to have taken place tomorrow will be turned into a conference."

And two days later: "Last night at the

Grand Hotel, Manchester, a conference was held between the Lancashire County Committee and the senior clubs. The latter organisation had made a request that the working of the Senior Competition be left in their own hands and the County Committee refused to accede. Most of the senior clubs refused to attend the annual meeting of secretaries, to arrange fixtures, called the previous Tuesday." The result was a mass resignation of the senior clubs.

The senior clubs in Yorkshire and Lancashire actively sought other clubs to join them. Their plan was to implement a Lancashire Northern Union League and a Yorkshire Northern Union League with the winners of each playing-off for the right to call themselves champions of the Northern Union. This was a plan which had been mooted, on and off, for a number of years and which had been submitted to the Rugby Union as late as 1895.

The senior clubs were under the impression that they had only resigned from their respective county bodies and were still members of the English Rugby Union. This belief was quickly dispelled, as Old Ebor pointed out: "But the great mistake of all was to resign membership of the Yorkshire Union and to attempt to shelter themselves under the wing of the parent body. Those who advised this step now seem astonished to find that membership of the English Union entails acknowledgement of the county Union's authority. They can perhaps now understand the readiness with which the English Union accepted their fees of membership. It seemed a simple act to hand over their subscriptions but in reality it was handing over every vestige of independence left to them, for it gave the English Union and through that body the Yorkshire Union just the far reaching control which the two latter bodies must, in their secret hearts have desired."

Finding themselves isolated, the rebel Lancashire and Yorkshire clubs found a great reluctance on the part of others to join them. The senior clubs seemed only to be concerned with their own interests. To make matters worse, all was not peace and harmony within their own ranks, as demonstrated by a series of articles which appeared in the *Lancashire Daily Post* during August 1895.

On Tuesday 20 August that newspaper reported a meeting held the previous evening by the Yorkshire clubs to discuss the possibility of re-joining the Yorkshire Union: "The bulk of the clubs were in favour of fighting the matter to the bitter end and forming a Northern Union. It is, however, certain that Leeds, Bradford, Huddersfield and Halifax will not agree to such a course and it was reported that the Lancashire clubs generally were opposed to the project."

And the following day: "The decision of the Yorkshire "discontents" to send a deputation to discuss the position of affairs with the Yorkshire Rugby Union has been well received in Lancashire and has given great satisfaction. The Lancashire clubs which seceded from the First Class Championship have regretted their actions....It is now likely that the whole thing will be patched up before the season commences."

At this stage there were eight Yorkshire clubs supporting the idea of a breakaway and four opposed. In the middle were nine Lancashire clubs which, while regretting leaving the Union, were prepared, if necessary, to support the Yorkshire clubs in the formation of a Northern Union.

On 23 August the *Lancashire Daily Post* commented: "The opinion in Yorkshire is that within a week the Northern Rugby League will be an accomplished fact. The clubs will comprise the seniors of Yorkshire and Lancashire, who will sever from the parent body and make their own laws, including payment for broken-time. Leeds, Huddersfield and Bradford have declined to join and the three best Yorkshire Second Competition clubs will probably be invited to join, but failing this, the card will be filled up with Lancashire clubs."

This article confirms that the original idea had been to form two separate county leagues and shows the split in the ranks of the Yorkshire clubs, even at this late stage in the proceedings. For the first time in the debate, the issue of broken-time payments was mentioned.

The Lancashire Daily Post of 27 August had news of fresh developments. The report confirms that the senior clubs had already resigned from the Union and, therefore, did not resign at the meeting on 29 August held in Huddersfield: "At a meeting of the Yorkshire Rugby Union held at the Green Dragon Hotel, Leeds last evening it was decided that a deputation should not be appointed to meet six representatives of the late Senior Competition for the purposes of discussing the present situation in rugby football in Yorkshire. But that the senior clubs' deputation should be invited to meet the whole County Committee on Monday 9 September. It was pointed out during the lengthy discussions which ensued on the matter that, as the senior clubs were not now members of the Yorkshire Union, the latter body was not compelled to receive any deputation."

The senior clubs were now isolated "unable to run the risk of being left out in the cold" (though Dewsbury pulled out at the last minute). The Leeds club, initially opposed to the breakaway, held a committee meeting on 26 August, the same evening that the Yorkshire Rugby Union met. Leeds decided to join the Northern Union, fearful of being left behind. It was under these circumstances that the clubs met at the George Hotel, Huddersfield on 29 August 1895. Two Cheshire clubs, Runcorn and Stockport, also entered the equation. High on the agenda was the requirement for a fixture list for the coming season. At this meeting the clubs arranged fixtures among themselves, eventually playing each other home and away, to make a total of 42 matches. A Northern Union was officially formed thereby enabling member clubs to control their own financial situation. It was decided to begin the season earlier than the Rugby Union and the principle of paying players six shillings for broken-time was officially accepted.

The twenty-two clubs comprised Broughton Rangers, Leigh, Oldham, Rochdale Hornets, St Helens, Tyldesley, Warrington, Widnes and Wigan from Lancashire, Batley, Bradford, Brighouse Rangers, Halifax, Huddersfield, Hull, Hunslet, Leeds, Liversedge, Manningham and Wakefield Trinity from Yorkshire and Cheshire clubs Runcorn and Stockport.

The Northern Union was clearly not formed with the issue of broken-time at the forefront. There were many other more important reasons behind the breakaway. Looked at in this light the meeting at the George Hotel takes on a different perspective, which suggests it was not called necessarily to breakaway from the Rugby Union but rather to attempt to organise fixtures. The clubs had seen for themselves the success of the Football League, which had progressed steadily and now included two divisions each of 16 clubs. This had been achieved within the confines of the ruling body, the Football Association. They did not anticipate, at this stage, that the split from the Rugby Union was anything other than a temporary state of affairs.

The breakaway clubs were overtaken by events and put in a position they could never have anticipated. They took no responsibility for the development of the game. If the Rugby Union's major fault was that it was too detached from the clubs, the Northern Union suffered because it was run entirely by the clubs. It was too insular. There is no real evidence that the original twenty-two clubs actively sought to increase membership; they simply sat back and waited for it to happen which, slowly but surely, it did, spreading throughout Cumberland, Westmorland, Durham and Northumberland.

No doubt many of the administrators of the Northern Union were worthy men but their horizons appeared to be narrow, their vision parochial. They failed to see that without the solid foundation provided by junior clubs their own existence was imperilled. Of the original 22 clubs, five (Brighouse Rangers,

Liversedge, Manningham, Stockport and Tyldesley) had dropped out by 1906; Runcorn survived up to the Great War. In the first decade of the century, eleven fresh clubs, including six from Wales, were, at various times, members of the Northern Union major league. None survived beyond 1913. This lack of foundation has been at the root of Rugby League's inability to spread its wings in Britain.

The smaller clubs were left with no real alternative but to join the Northern Union but the majority were unable to pay broken-time and, failing to swim in the big pond, failed to survive. The Northern Union was hastily thrown together and it showed. It should be remembered that though the newly constituted Northern Union had major problems, the Rugby Union was decimated and many decades were to pass before it could approach its former eminence.

The Battle for Survival

Following the turmoil of the summer of 1895, the Northern Union got down to the business of playing rugby. The events, which are often now referred to as the "great schism", were not viewed in that light by the Northern press which simply reported both Northern Union and Rugby Union under the single heading of football. They appeared to regard the split as a temporary state of affairs.

Before the split the clubs had evolved a natural financial balance. They cut their cloth according to their means over a period of time. This delicate balance was, to a large extent, destroyed. It must have come as a shock to find that the Rugby Union would no longer turn a blind eye to the issue of broken-time. The breakaway clubs thought they had the strength of Lancashire and Yorkshire behind them and never imagined the Rugby Union would react in the way it did.

The effect of the breakaway on the clubs left out of the original select bunch of twenty-two is best illustrated by examining the fortunes of the teams which were to make up the Lancashire Second Competition. Their situation, far from being unique, was typical of the position all clubs in the North were faced with following the action taken by the seniors.

A myth which has developed regarding this period in the game's history is that clubs flocked to join the Northern Union and that all embraced it with great enthusiasm. On the face of it the growing number of clubs joining the Northern Union appears to support that view but the reality is a little different.

With the breakaway the Rugby Union structure in Lancashire was decimated. Clubs were promoted into leagues which were too strong for them in playing terms and, more importantly, placed them in a situation where the costs, particularly travelling expenses, were dramatically increased. Inevitably, most clubs began to experience financial difficulties. These were exacerbated when support began to decline mainly because of uneven contests and fixtures against opposition regarded as unattractive.

During previous seasons the junior clubs would have played a number of lucrative friendly fixtures against the senior clubs. Walkden, for example, relied upon a visit from Swinton, Barton one from Salford and so on. If the weather was kind and the clubs involved playing well with every chance of an upset, then a good-sized crowd could be expected to watch the contest. The junior clubs' share of such gate receipts meant the difference between ending the season with a profit or loss.

The junior clubs, facing financial instability, inevitably followed the senior clubs in the hope that the fixtures would return. These junior clubs, in turn, played fixtures against clubs smaller than themselves. Lancaster, for example, would play the likes of Kendal Hornets, Askam, Dalton or Ambleside. Once again such fixtures ensured the survival of this next level. The knock-on effect was severe, for if a club such as Barton or Ulverston, Morecambe or Walkden, were to lose just one club from its fixture list to the Northern Union, it then had two empty dates to fill. Inevitably, the clubs found it increasingly difficult to function within the Rugby Union and so the slow trickle of defecting clubs became a steady stream as more clubs strived to obtain fixtures which would attract them support.

The Lancashire Rugby Union committee's decision to abolish the now inoperable league system and return to friendly fixtures for the 1897-98 season helped them not at all. For many clubs this was the last straw and they were forced to turn to the Northern Union in order to survive. Pensee, writing in the *Lancaster Guardian* on 17 April 1897, had this to say:

"From all accounts, the North Lancashire clubs have had quite enough of the Rugby Union and it will not be surprising if they do not at the end of the season go over in a body to the Northern Union. The past season at Barrow has been a most disastrous one, there not having been the slightest interest in the club's doings for some time. During the week a petition, numerously signed, has been presented to the club to call a special meeting to consider the advisability of joining the Northern Union.....Millom will do the same for the "gates" got from Cumberland clubs will not keep the club going....The fact is that football clubs nowadays equal such a large expenditure that substantial "gates" are an absolute necessity if a club is to pay its way and unfortunately the public does not seem to take the same interest in friendly matches that they take in encounters where the loss or gain of a couple of points in a competition is involved. That has been the experience at Lancaster for the "gates" at even the most important of friendly matches....have been far from satisfactory...."

The Lancaster club was not slow in following up Pensee's view. On 1 May 1897 it was reported that a meeting had been called by the club and it had been decided to join the Northern Union. What is surprising to note are some of the reasons put forward by people at that meeting and just how essential they felt such a move was for the survival of the club:

"Mr Walter Brockbank: he was convinced that a much better card (fixture list) could be put forward for next season than they had under the Rugby Union. He thought it would be better for them financially. Their fixture list last season, with the exception of half a dozen matches, was very poor and took them back ten years....

"Mr Ball: with regard to finances; they had a number of vice-presidents who subscribed liberally to their funds. He rather thought some of those gentlemen would not see their way to support a club which was a sort of semi-professional business....He had no great objection to paying a man broken-time but the Northern Union went further than that....they would need to pay some of their players if not all.....it was a costly business to pay their players 30 shillings per week...."

Lancaster joined the growing number of clubs going over to the Northern Union simply to stop the club from going out of existence. Not all were in agreement and a number of committee men and vice-presidents resigned rather than join what they referred to as "the broken-time brigade". Lancaster had great difficulty in finding people to fill the positions of treasurer and secretary.

It was a similar situation further north. *The Barrow News* of 24 April 1897 carried news of the Barrow club's decision to go over.

"Mr Keighley said, before reading the resolution, he would like to say that he and other members felt disappointment with the talent catered for the public during the past season and, more importantly, at the very poor gates....he, for one, would like the club to remain members of the Rugby Union if it were found possible to carry on the club successfully...."

It is illuminating to note the resolution put to that meeting: "We, the members of the Barrow Rugby Football Club, in general meeting here assembled do hereby resolve to join the Northern Union and that it be an instruction to our secretary to take the necessary steps to obtain admission into the above Union immediately."

It was the members, rather than the players or the committee, who desired change. When the vote was called only two hands were raised against it but some members of the committee resigned in protest.

Ulverston, on the other hand, had resolved at their AGM in 1897 to remain loyal to the Rugby Union. Undoubtedly, a major reason for this decision was a visit from Mr Higson, the then secretary of the Lancashire County Rugby Union, who laid before them plans for a Lancashire, Cheshire and Cumberland League which, he claimed, was to come into effect the following season.

This League, Mr Higson assured the meeting, would adequately cater for the needs of the Ulverston club. Suitably impressed, the meeting voted to remain in the Rugby Union. However, the new League failed to materialise and when Ulverston's secretary travelled to Manchester for the annual meeting to arrange fixtures he was unable to obtain a single one. None of the Rugby Union clubs wished to travel to Ulverston. The *Barrow News* of 3 July 1897 carried a report of an Extraordinary General Meeting called by the Ulverston club to consider the future in light of recent events:

"....the chairman, in opening the proceedings, said they were in no doubt aware why that special meeting had been called. Most of them were present at the annual meeting when the county secretary and other county officials gave their views on the Northern Union versus the Rugby Union....as the only alternative....the meeting had been convened to consider whether the club should be disbanded altogether or should they go over to the Northern Union...."

According to the report Ulverston had already been in contact with the Northern Union and had been referred to Mr Ellison, the secretary of the newly formed Lancashire Second Competition. At the meeting the Ulverston secretary read a telegram he had received that day which stated: "Millom has officially applied to join the second division today."

This was greeted with great enthusiasm by the assembled men, following which, it was reported: "Mr W Hull, amidst applause, moved that the club be not disbanded but they join the Northern Union at once...."

The meeting indicated just how far-reaching the existence of illegal payments for broken-time had been. Broken-time payments had, most certainly, reached the north of the county for the report went on "Having sounded out the players he (Mr Hull) had found they were willing to play on the old terms. It is no secret to those with a knowledge of the innermost workings of the club that for some years it had been the practice to pay their players for time actually lost (laughter and cries of "Oh?!!")."

The motion was carried unanimously as it was felt that rugby with the Northern Union was the only choice. However, even under these circumstances, there were some who still felt the disloyalty shown to the Rugby Union was too much. Two elected members of the committee resigned and the club president, Mr Myles Kennedy, "declined to continue under the new auspices."

It was a similar story with another prominent club in this part of the world, Millom. A fierce local rival of the Ulverston club, Millom decided to switch to the Northern Union and the *Barrow News* of 6 July 1897 carried official notification. Millom had found itself in the same position as Ulverston at the Manchester meeting of fixture secretaries. According to the report, it had been successful in attracting only "third rate" clubs to play. A meeting had been called to discuss the situation and the chairman had outlined the options available in very blunt terms:

"They had the choice of three things: to give up football in Millom altogether, to remain in the Rugby Union and take part in the Cumberland League or go to the Northern Union."

Millom could not survive on the gates being attracted by playing clubs from Cumberland so that was not really an option. Giving the game up was not what any rugby enthusiast, in any age, would wish to do. In reality the Millom club had no choice other than to join the Lancashire Second Competition. This course of action was confirmed unanimously by club members at the meeting.

Moving further south a slightly different story emerges. Fleetwood had been formed specifically to play the new game of Northern Union football and thus did not have a history of playing Rugby Union. The major driving force behind the Fleetwood club was undoubtedly a Welshman, D Bowen Evans, who in addition to being the club's first captain was also the treasurer of the newly formed Lancashire Second Competition. Evans represented the club at the meeting in Manchester when the Second Competition was inaugurated. Fleetwood, an exceptional case it would seem, conforms to the accepted view of clubs which flocked to the Northern Union banner.

Another club which took this route was Birkenhead Wanderers which was not struggling at all and, quite to the contrary, had just completed a most successful season. What prompted it to join the Northern Union was something entirely different, the chance of glory.

The club had lived in the shadow of the much larger and more successful Birkenhead Park, playing its home matches about half a mile from its rival's ground, hence Wanderers' nickname of the "little 'uns." For the Wanderers club it opened up the possibility of becoming the top Northern Union side on the Wirral. This was the most important factor behind the decision to change allegiance.

An investigation into the clubs which were based in the heartland of the game, the Manchester clubs, reveals similar reasons with the over-riding one being the need to ensure survival. Radcliffe, one of Lancashire's oldest established clubs, may be taken as a typical example of this decision making process. At a special meeting of the committee, held at the town's Rams Head Hotel on 18 May 1896, it was decided by a unanimous vote to join the Northern Union.

"We were compelled to make the step" an unnamed member of the committee was reported to have stated in the *Bury Times*. "If we had stayed where we were we would have played only junior clubs who run, punt, bury your head off and don't play the game."

The club had few doubts about the wisdom of the decision, not that there was much of a choice to make. "If we are to die we might as well die under Northern Union rules" the committee man continued.

An added factor was the longer playing season with a start at the beginning of September and a finish at the end of April. Previously, the Rugby Union campaign had begun three weeks later and finished one week sooner.

The kick-off time under the Northern Union rules would, it was stated, be at a fixed time each week instead of the haphazard system which previously operated. Spectators would know when matches would start instead of waiting for anything up to two hours after the advertised kick-off time.

It was reported that neighbouring clubs such as Rochdale St Clement's, Walkden, Crompton and Werneth had made the decision to switch to the new body and that at the latest meeting of the Lancashire County Rugby Union the representatives of only five clubs were in attendance.

The widely held view that clubs rushed to join the Northern Union is not substantiated. Evidence suggests that many clubs were reluctant to leave the Rugby Union but were forced to do so through circumstance.

"Spectator power" was an important factor in clubs' thinking. Rugby supporters were used to watching league games and did not attend in anything like the same numbers for friendlies. "It is the battle for two league points which serves to whet the appetite of the football enthusiast" confirmed the *Bury Times*. Without competitive action, spectators stayed away or, in many areas, were attracted to the rival football code, soccer.

Having joined the Northern Union, newcomers were left to fend for themselves with virtually no support, financial or otherwise, from the senior clubs. The senior clubs looked after themselves to the detriment of the game itself.

Hindsight suggests that the senior clubs

had never envisaged the need for a structure for a game seemingly already established. There was no framework in place, or even thought of, to develop a strategy for expansion. The speed of events of the summer of 1895 pushed matters out of control and allowed no time to accommodate the junior clubs. Without a coherent plan the early years of the Northern Union were marked by a battle for survival.

These points are further elaborated in the following chapters.

The Lancashire Second Competition

THE formation of a Lancashire Second Competition was first officially mooted at a meeting of the Lancashire section of the Northern Union held in Manchester on 20 April 1897. Applications were invited by 20 May.

The response was such that both a Second and Third Competition were formed at a meeting in Manchester on 25 May 1897.

Originally the Second Competition was to comprise: Barrow, Lancaster, Birkenhead Wanderers, St Helens Recs, Crompton, Walkden, Radcliffe, Barton, Fleetwood and Dukinfield.

The Third Competition included: Altrincham, Werneth, Blackley Rangers, Leigh Shamrocks, Whitworth, Mossley, Rochdale Rangers, Cheetham Hill, Warrington St Mary's and Boothstown.

Subsequently, Millom and Ulverston were invited to join the Second Competition and Altrincham was promoted to fill the place left vacant upon Dukinfield closing down.

Blackley Rangers and Cheetham Hill failed to make the start of the season, both clubs having disbanded. Todmorden joined the Third Competition which began with eight clubs in membership. This was reduced to six during the 1897-98 season with both Boothstown and Mossley withdrawing.

1897-98

Crompton and St Helens Recs disbanded during the season and their results were expunged from the table. Barrow and Millom finished level on points and played-off for the championship. Barrow won 2-0 at Lancaster after the first game, at Askam, had finished scoreless. Barrow lost to Morecambe, bottom of the Senior Competition, in the test match at Lancaster.

Werneth won the Third Competition which lasted for only one season.

1898-99

Blackpool joined the Second Competition but Barton and Walkden disbanded during the season and their results were expunged from the table. Millom became "champions" and won promotion to the Senior Competition by defeating Morecambe in the test match. Altrincham, Barton, Blackpool, Fleetwood and Radcliffe, together with Werneth and Whitworth, formed a South East Lancashire League which lasted for only one season. Radcliffe was the champion club of the South East Lancashire League.

1899-1900

Relegated Morecambe joined the Second Competition alongside Dalton, Werneth and Whitworth. With Blackpool having disbanded eleven clubs began the season. Barrow won promotion to the Senior Competition by defeating Tyldesley in the test match. Werneth, Whitworth and Radcliffe, together with Todmorden, Hebden Bridge, Rochdale Rangers and Luddendenfoot formed a Border Towns League, won by Werneth. This competition lasted only for one season.

1900-01

Relegated Tyldesley and Leigh Shamrocks were the newcomers though, with Ulverston and Dalton having reverted to the amateur ranks, the season began with only ten clubs. This number was reduced to nine when Fleetwood disbanded during the season. Morecambe, the "champions", lost to Widnes in the test match.

This was the last season of the Second

Competition, the organisation being wound up at a meeting in Manchester on 23 July 1901.

With fourteen Lancashire and Yorkshire clubs having formed their own Northern League, Morecambe, Birkenhead Wanderers, Lancaster, Altrincham and Radcliffe were promoted to the Lancashire Senior Competition. Tyldesley and Whitworth disbanded, Werneth joined the Lancashire Combination and Leigh Shamrocks joined the Central Lancashire League.

Altrincham

FOUNDED: mid-1880's
CEASED: 1902
REASON: financial problems
GROUND: Devisdale, Bowdon
HEADQUARTERS: Foresters Arms
COLOURS: Red

ALTRINCHAM delayed the decision to join the Northern Union longer than most other clubs and, in the end, appeared to be faced with little alternative. The clamour of clubs rushing to join the new organisation was such that Altrincham faced increasing problems in finding opponents and the final straw came in March 1897 when it was left with only one remaining fixture, against Birkenhead Wanderers, before the end of the season due to the defections from the Rugby Union ranks.

The decision to join the Northern Union appears to have been forced upon the Altrincham committee and was not reported with any great enthusiasm but, having done the deed, it was determined to make the best of it. "Altrincham have at last taken the plunge and transferred their allegiance to the Northern Union" reported the *Altrincham Guardian*. Their opening game was a friendly at home to Walkden on 3 April 1897 when Altrincham won a "hotly contested" game 10-3.

Altrincham was one of only four clubs, the others being Radcliffe, Lancaster and Birkenhead Wanderers, to complete four seasons in the Lancashire Second Competition and yet the club very nearly began life in the third-class ranks. The Altrincham representative was present at the meeting which formed the Third Competition in May 1897 and then the club was promoted, without playing a match, to the second rank to replace Dukinfield.

Altrincham's home was at Devisdale, a large piece of spare land to the south-west of the town, actually situated in neighbouring Bowdon. The land was owned by the Earl of Stamford who let it to the Altrincham Agricultural Society and the rugby club was a sub-tenant. The lease was renewed annually, not always without question, as some of the Society members objected to "the coarse language of the footballers and their followers" and the rugby club was made to feel unimportant in many respects.

The ground was only free for football when the last of the summer shows had been completed and, as a result, Altrincham invariably had to play its first few games of the season away from home. Occasionally during the season the ground was unavailable so some games were played on a field off Stockport Road.

Altrincham began life in the Second Competition with a 6-10 defeat at Walkden, Harry Barnett and Fields scoring tries, and suffered further setbacks at Birkenhead Wanderers and St Helens Recs before a 7-3 win at Crompton gave heart. The Birkenhead game was noteworthy for the fact that heavy rain caused the dye in Altrincham's red jerseys to run. The Birkenhead players, attired in white, were soon covered in red and the teams became virtually indistinguishable.

It was not until 23 October that the team played its first home league game losing 3-8 to Ulverston. Altrincham, on its day, could match most sides but frequently disappointed its supporters. Altrincham did achieve a notable home and away success against championship-chasing Millom and gave a creditable display against senior club Salford in the Challenge Cup losing 0-16 at Devisdale after a brave fight. Altrincham's refusal to switch the tie to Salford was justified by a ground record crowd of around 3000.

THE RUGBY LEAGUE MYTH

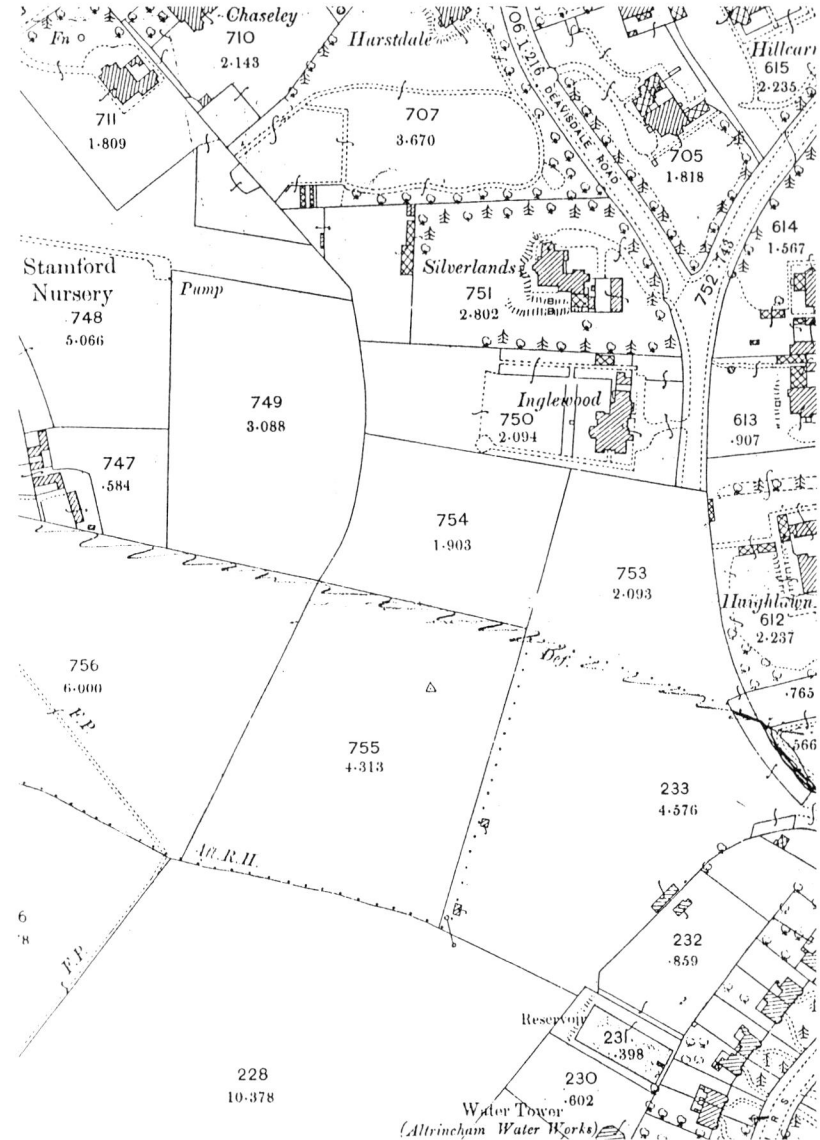

Altrincham played on a large piece of spare land off Devisdale (spelt Deavisdale on this map) Road. The playing pitch was in the area of the map references 232 and 233. (Reproduced from 1893 Ordnance Survey Map, courtesy of Cheshire County Council Archives and Local Studies)

"The first season of Northern Union football has been satisfactory" reported the *Altrincham Guardian*. "Financially the club is on the wrong side....but interest has been maintained." The deficit was around £20.

Harry Barnett won Cheshire honours during the season and in subsequent years F Fields, S Hanson, J Findlow and P Wilkinson all played in a county side dominated by Runcorn and Stockport representatives.

The following season, 1898-99, brought a significant improvement as Altrincham finished an eventual fifth despite a falling-off in form towards the end of the campaign. The club was unbeaten in its opening five games despite four of them being played away. It turned out in new colours, chocolate and sky blue hoops replacing the traditional red.

Though finding league rugby a struggle at times, Altrincham appeared to have avoided some of the financial problems which afflicted some of its rivals and found some of its neighbours always ready to lend a hand. Senior clubs such as Widnes, Stockport and Runcorn played regular friendly games, often attracting some of Devisdale's best gates of the season.

Altrincham's inconsistency again reared its ugly head in 1899-1900, with a good start, including wins at Radcliffe and Morecambe, being followed by some poor displays. Late in the season Altrincham did reveal attacking flair, notably in a 32-0 home win over Whitworth, but eventually slipped to a disappointing sixth.

A firm decision had been taken by the committee to field local players and dispense with outsiders who had been on good terms. "The present team are not a highly paid fifteen" reported the *Altrincham Guardian*. The policy seemed to be paying off as the club was reported to be much better placed in a financial sense. "It will be a new experience for a Second Competition team to be out of debt and unless something is done to curtail the enormous travelling expenses this sore point will remain....the senior clubs growl at the journey to Millom. What would they say if this was multiplied to five as with the Second Competition clubs?" asked the local reporter.

It was stated that the Second Competition clubs had appealed to the senior clubs for financial assistance but that this was refused at a General Committee Meeting of the Northern Union.

In 1900-01, the last season of the Second Competition, Altrincham suffered like fellow members from the sparsity of fixtures and had completed all but one of the 16 league games by the end of January. After opening the season with four defeats, Altrincham enjoyed a run of only one defeat in the next ten games and finally finished fourth. To great disappointment, though, the club went out of the Challenge Cup at the first hurdle losing to Cumbrian side, Aspatria. A long and expensive journey, made at considerable loss, might have been worthwhile if progress in the competition had been made but a 3-4 defeat made for a miserable return home.

The club emerged from the Second Competition relatively unscathed despite the recurrent problems of high travel costs, made worse by its location, and payments for broken-time. Yet, ironically, it was the team's elevation into the senior ranks which was to lead to problems. In the 1901-02 season the league system was revamped and Altrincham was one of five Second Competition clubs promoted to the Lancashire Senior Competition.

The problems began before a ball was kicked when the thorny problem of players' registration came to the fore. Players had been allowed to hold a dual registration for a first-class and second-class club but with all clubs now being on the same level this distinction was ended. Much to Altrincham's dismay the authorities ruled that, in the event of a dual registration, the player be regarded as belonging to the club which had in the previous season been in the first-class ranks.

Many of Altrincham's players fell into this category, even though their appearances in senior ranks were often infrequent. At a stroke the club was denied the services of Hanson and Fields (registered by Salford), Findlow (Bradford), Wilkinson and Chorlton (Swinton) and Royle and Deakin (Warrington). Though some active recruitment policy led to the acquisition of some useful players, including Stott, the impressive half-back from the now-defunct Whitworth club and a Swansea forward by the name of McKrill, the team was undoubtedly on the light side. To further depress the committee, Altrincham had two points deducted for fielding an ineligible player.

Apart from facing the former Second Competition clubs, Altrincham was clearly out of its depth at the higher level and won only two of the 26 league games with another being drawn. In all, a total of twelve of the previous season's players failed to reappear in the Altrincham ranks and, despite the inclusion of a steady stream of new recruits, results were disastrous.

The club's financial problems worsened and the players appeared less than sympathetic. Often a scratch side had to be gathered together as first-teamers refused to play at short notice and, lacking a strong second string, Altrincham suffered some heavy reverses.

The local reporter, reviewing the season in the *Altrincham Guardian*, had clearly had enough. "It has been a season of disaster" he wrote. "In addition to the team not displaying anything like the cleverness accustomed to, there are the financial embarrassments the club has had to face all along the line and, as if to complete the already too numerous obstacles, a not too happy relationship between the players and those in authority."

Many players simply deserted the club when the money began to run out and, despite often being praised for their "plucky displays", many of the games were foregone conclusions.

Swinton, a senior club which, unlike many of its rivals, was always ready to lend a helping hand to neighbouring clubs in difficulties, played a friendly at Devisdale in an attempt to raise funds. The match, played on Good Friday 28 March 1902, attracted a fair crowd but any money raised was soon swallowed up by the mounting debts.

Sadly, this proved to be the final home game in Altrincham's history and the club folded soon after the end of the season. The meagre assets were sold at auction in November 1902.

Barrow

FOUNDED: 1875
GROUND: Cavendish Park
HEADQUARTERS: Royal Hotel, Strand
COLOURS: Red and black

BARROW'S formation came at a time when the town was developing quickly into one of the largest industrial centres in the country. In the early days Barrow played at two venues, Cavendish Park and the Parade Ground, before the former got the vote as the club's permanent home.

Games against neighbouring towns and villages such as Ulverston, Millom and Askam always attracted good crowds and a fierce rivalry. Morecambe and Lancaster were also regular opponents but, by the early 1880's, Barrow had gained fixtures against many of the top sides in Lancashire and Yorkshire. The town's geographical isolation was compensated to a degree by an excellent railway service.

Barrow was elected to membership of the Lancashire Rugby Union on 12 November 1884 and its first representative honour came a year later when forward W Kinnish was chosen to play for Lancashire against Cheshire. He was followed into the county side by a number of Barrovians over the next few years.

One of the largest crowds seen at Cavendish Park, around 6000, saw a local district side beat the touring Maoris in the 1888-89 season. The receipts of £120 easily met the tourists' guarantee.

Barrow competed in the North-Western League from its formation and received an enormous boost when invited to fill St Helens Recs' place in the First Class ranks of the Lancashire Club Championship in its second season, 1893-94, Recs having decided to play friendly games only.

League games home and away against Oldham, Swinton, Warrington, Wigan, Tyldesley, Salford, Broughton Rangers, Rochdale Hornets and Broughton created a great deal of interest in the town and increased the club's prestige enormously. Sadly, however, Barrow finished one place off the bottom of the table gaining only three wins and three draws in 18 games.

As such they had to play Leigh, who finished runners-up in the Second Class Competition, in a test match at Wigan for the right to compete in the top rank in 1894-95. Leigh won by two tries to nil and so, after only one season, Barrow was relegated.

Undaunted, Barrow soon recovered and enjoyed a marvellous season in what became known as "the two cups year." Inspired by half-back Sam Northmore, who had joined the club for a short spell from its great rival Millom, Barrow won the Second Class Championship, winning 15 of its 16 games, conceding only two goals and one try throughout the league campaign. Barrow also won the North-Western League, losing only one out of 12 league games finishing seven points clear of "runners-up" Millom.

In 1895-96 Barrow was again in the First Class ranks but, due to the large number of defections to the Northern Union, found the competition vastly downgraded in importance. Apart from games against the likes of Morecambe, Lancaster, Swinton and Salford, many of Barrow's opponents were hardly great drawing cards and hence gate money, a subject of increasing importance to all clubs especially those with large travelling costs to meet, was down on previous seasons.

A notable honour was bestowed upon the club when forward George Hughes was chosen to play for England against Scotland in March 1896.

THE RUGBY LEAGUE MYTH

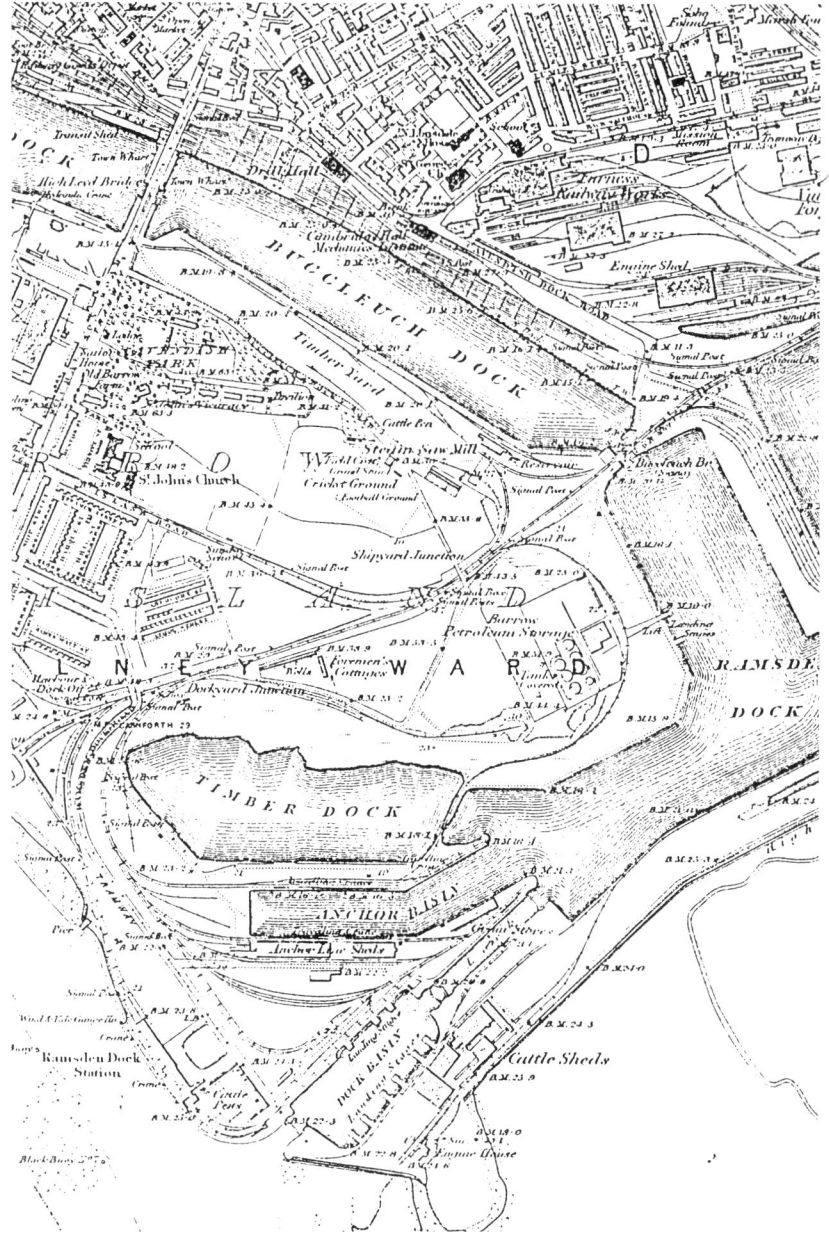

Barrow's Cavendish Park ground was in close proximity to the docks. (Reproduced from the 1893 Ordnance Survey Map.)

A Lancashire Rugby Union team line-up from 1895-96 season including 3 players, Pinch, Hughes and Holmes, who went on to play in the Lancashire Second Competition.
Back row: W B Stoddart, G G Allen, R Pierce (all Liverpool), J Pinch (Lancaster), S Walsh (Pemberton), R Moss (Salford). **Middle row:** W Mainwaring (Salford), G H Murray, J Valentine (both Swinton), G E Hughes (Barrow), J Jones (Swinton). **Front row:** R Holmes (Morecambe), R Lewis (Liverpool), J T Lewis (Swinton), W Parlane (Manchester). (Photograph courtesy Tim Auty)

Barrow's last season in the Rugby Union, in 1896-97, was an eventful one. With the departure of many of the top sides in the county to the breakaway Northern Union a number of Barrow players formed the nucleus of the Lancashire side. F Wildman, T Bowker, R Bell and Hughes all featured regularly in the county side while W Cunningham, who later in the season joined Millom, played for Cumberland and G Whitwell represented Westmorland.

Further recognition came when Cavendish Park was chosen as a venue for a county championship game for the first time when Lancashire played Cumberland on 28 November 1896.

Events were moving so quickly, however, that on 20 April 1897 the "almost unanimous" decision was taken to join the Northern Union at a special meeting of the club held at the Central Hall. Before the season was out, Barrow played its first games under the new banner, defeating Morecambe and Wigan at Cavendish Park.

Barrow was a natural choice for inclusion in the Second Competition and the club's officials were involved in all the discussions leading to its formation. No sooner had Barrow joined the new set-up than the immediate ambition was to move upwards. With the increasing costs of travel and a new factor, broken-time, to contend with the committee realised that competing in the league would lead to a big drain on resources. Promotion to the senior ranks, bringing with it the prospect of more attractive opposition, was seen as a pressing priority.

Barrow's first season in the Northern Union was a successful one and the club became involved in an exciting race for the championship with neighbouring Millom. Barrow won all of its home games and appeared well in control when a body-blow was struck with the decision of St Helens Recs to follow Crompton's lead and disband late in the season.

Barrow had beaten St Helens Recs away while Millom had suffered two defeats against Recs. The decision of the league executive to expunge Recs' results from the league table threw an entirely different light on things and Millom, by defeating Barrow 7-0 in the final league game, tied for the championship.

Barrow had merrily concerned itself with plans for a game against a Rest of the League side and preparations for the test match under the false impression that the league would be decided on scoring average in the event of two clubs finishing level on points. Barrow had scored 237 points and conceded 59 while Millom's record was far inferior, 173 against 55. Millom protested against this presumption and the Northern Union came down in Millom's favour and ordered the clubs to play-off for the championship.

The Boilermakers, as Barrow was known at the time, finally saw off their rivals after the first game, at Askam, had finished scoreless. Barrow won the replay, staged at Quay Meadow, Lancaster in terrible conditions of wind and rain, with a goal kicked by Proctor late in the game following a mark by Treweek.

A week later Barrow was again at Quay Meadow, for the test against Morecambe. Perhaps exertions of the previous weeks had caught up with them for Barrow failed to show anything like the usual form and went down to a 0-10 defeat thus losing out on the chance of a senior place.

Figures released at the club's AGM demonstrated the wisdom of switching codes. Gate money totalled £284, an increase of £148 on the previous season, though railway fares (£130) and payments for broken-time (£67) were significant items.

In 1898-99 Barrow played second fiddle to Millom which dropped only one point on the way to the championship. As runners-up Barrow trailed in six points behind. Despite this, the townsfolk's enthusiasm for the game remained undiminished with practice sessions regularly attracting crowds of two and three hundred and most home gates hovering around the three thousand mark.

It took the Barrow club three seasons to finally realise its ambitions when, in 1899-1900, it was easily the best team in the Second Competition and won 17 games, drew two and lost only once to eventual runners-up Werneth. "There is not a drawing club in membership" was how the local reporter summed up the standard of opposition. "Barrow have attained what they have long struggled for" was his conclusion at the end of the season, "and their soaring ambitions have been realised."

Barrow ran up some high scores with Bawden, Bowker and Wharton the chief try-scorers and in the test match, at Lancaster, Barrow made no mistake. Barrow easily beat fallen giant Tyldesley 22-8 to claim its place in the senior ranks. The "red and blacks" had attained their long-awaited position in the top flight and, of all the teams which competed in the Second Competition, they were the only one to survive long-term as a senior, professional club.

Barrow was a major town and the team could be guaranteed a high level of support when enjoying a winning run. In its last season as a Second Competition club a crowd of 6000 saw Barrow lose narrowly at home to Bradford in the Challenge Cup. In Barrow's first season in the Lancashire Senior Competition gates showed a marked increase on previous campaigns. A crowd of 6000 was also recorded when Lancashire beat Cumberland 19-3, at Cavendish Park, in January 1902.

The history of Barrow has been detailed elsewhere and needs no further repetition here. Suffice to say that the club has experienced highs and lows, but throughout it all the town has remained a rugby stronghold with a firm foundation from the amateur ranks. Had the decision at that momentous meeting in April 1897 gone the other way and Barrow remained as a member of the Rugby Union, a game which was fast becoming a backwater in the north-west, or had Barrow not gained promotion as quickly as it did, the club's eventful history might well have followed a different path.

Within a few years of joining the Northern Union, Barrow's neighbours Ulverston, Dalton and Millom found they could no longer meet the financial demands of the new code. Barrow had a stronger financial base and greater potential and so emerged from the early years of the Northern Union relatively unscathed.

Barton

FOUNDED: early 1880's
CEASED: 1898
REASON: financial problems
GROUND: Tetlow Fold
HEADQUARTERS: Bridgewater Hotel, Patricroft
COLOURS: Red

BARTON was regarded as a junior club which, because of its location with Salford, Swinton and Broughton Rangers in close proximity, would struggle to rise through the ranks. In the first season of the Lancashire Second Competition, 1897-98, Barton achieved fleeting success before overspending had its inevitable consequences.

Situated five miles west of Manchester it was at Barton-upon-Irwell that in 1770 Brindley constructed an aqueduct to carry the Bridgewater Canal across the River Irwell. This gave place in 1893 to an aqueduct by which the canal was carried over the Manchester Ship Canal. The team's nickname was "*the Ship Canal lads*".

Barton was the centre of a rural district and had a population in the 1890's of only a few thousand though centres of much larger population were nearby.

It was in the 1891-92 season that the Barton club made its first impression on the rugby world, at least in local circles, defeating Failsworth in the final of the South East Lancashire Cup. The following season Barton finished top of the South East Lancashire League, a competition which also included Pendleton, Boothstown, Blackley Rangers, Failsworth, Radcliffe, Tottington, Manchester Athletic, Milnrow and Cheetham Hill, and retained the Cup, again defeating Failsworth in the final.

In 1893-94 the league system in Lancashire was extended from one to three divisions and Barton finished fourth in the Third Class Competition behind Blackley Rangers, Pendleton and Werneth. The following season, the last before the breakaway, Barton again attained fourth spot behind Pemberton, Crompton and Morecambe.

The mass defections led to Barton being upgraded to Second Class status in 1895-96. The destination of the championship was decided only on the last day of the season when Mossley gained the point needed and Barton ended joint "runners-up" alongside Radcliffe and Leigh Shamrocks.

Barton was one of ten clubs which formed a severely depleted First Class Competition in 1896-97, which was abandoned in March 1897 when Blackley Rangers, Leigh Shamrocks, Mossley and Barton decided to join the Northern Union. Barton's last game under the auspices of the Rugby Union was on 27 February 1897 when the ninth successive win was recorded in defeating Boothstown 12-4.

Two Barton forwards, J Johnson and J Hadcroft had achieved Lancashire county honours under Rugby Union rules, a fine achievement for a "village" club.

Barton's first match as a member of the Northern Union was on 13 March 1897 when the team beat Blackley Rangers at home 12-0 with tries by Grindley, Benyon, Robinson and Kelly. Eight more friendly games were played before the end of the season and Barton was encouraged by some fine results beating senior clubs Tyldesley, Stockport and Huddersfield, the latter at Fartown 6-4, a notable win which raised more than a few eyebrows.

As a founder member of the Lancashire Second Competition, Barton prepared for the testing campaign with some team strengthening, though where the money came from was a source of wonderment. Chief recruit was the brilliant half-back Buff Berry,

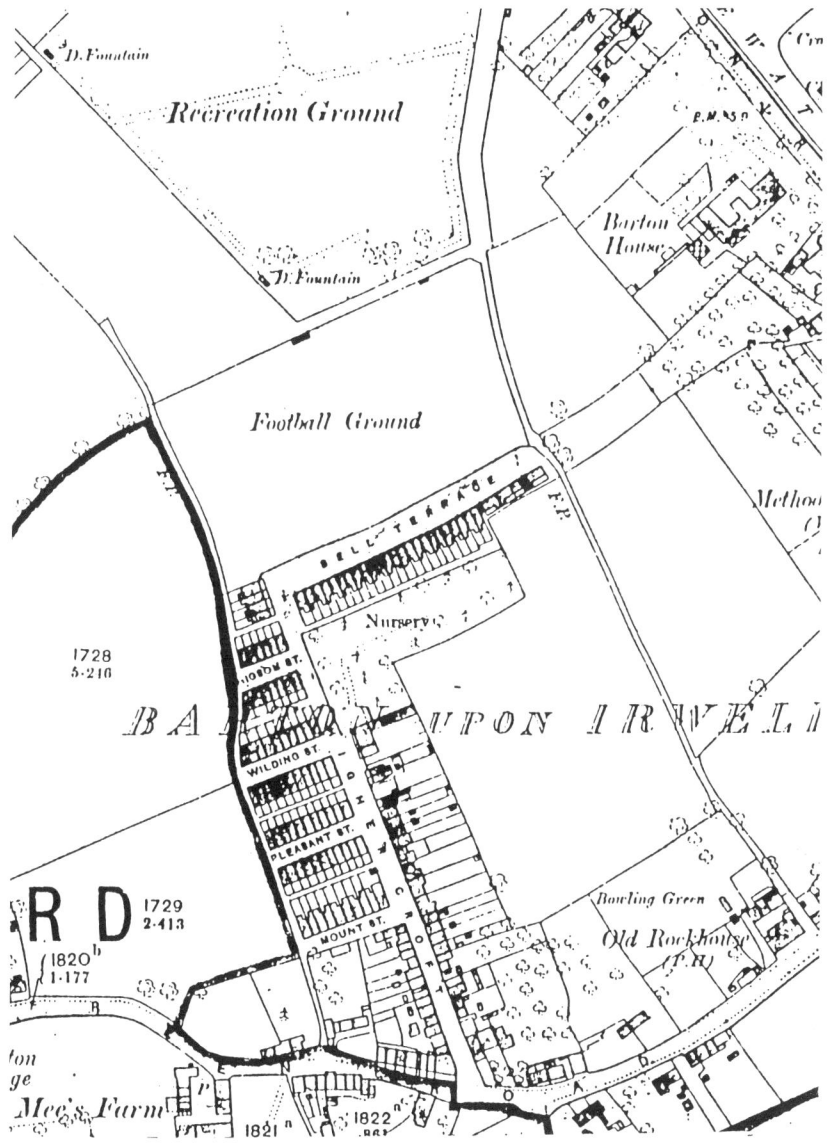

Barton's Tetlow Fold enclosure. (Reproduced from 1893 Ordnance Survey Map)

a former England Rugby Union international, who was enticed away from Tyldesley. "Buff was offered terms which the Tyldesley committee simply could not hope to match" concluded the *Leigh Journal*.

Despite the money spent on players, Barton's ground did not win many admiring comments. "After a five minutes walk from Patricroft station the Wanderers players found a rough and uneven field, lacking in herbage (grass)" commented the *Birkenhead News*.

Barton made a sensational start to its league career, taking a 9-0 interval lead over championship favourite Millom, on the opening day of the season. Though Millom recovered to win 15-9 Barton had announced its intentions.

Barton had assembled a talented side which played entertaining rugby. Berry brought with him a goal-kicking full-back, J Farrimond, who soon made an impact while winger Harry Grindley scored some spectacular tries. A number of Welshmen also found their way to Barton and the side was changing week-by-week.

Grindley scored two tries in a fine 18-10 win at Lancaster and in the following match a ground record crowd of around 4000 saw Barton inflict Barrow's first defeat 13-3. By January, Barton was regarded as a championship contender and a thrilling 5-3 home win over Millom, on 15 January, saw Barton reach the top of the league.

Success was to be short-lived, however, as Barton suffered a swift fall from grace losing each of the remaining five league games. Most ignominious of these was a defeat at Fleetwood, the *Wyresiders'* only league success of the season.

There was a brief respite from league problems as Barton reached the third round of the Challenge Cup with wins against Rochdale Rangers and Werneth. One of the largest crowds ever seen at Tetlow Fold, over 3000, saw Barton's cup hopes ended after a dour struggle, 3-9 at the hands of Bramley.

Rumours abounded that Barton's financial problems would result in the club disbanding but it was still functioning as the 1898-99 season opened. It was noticeable that there were many changes from the previous campaign in the side which lost 5-7 at home to Radcliffe. Berry had returned to his former stamping ground at Tyldesley and a number of the Welsh players were also absent. "Barton have lost several of last season's players and are playing mostly local men" commented the *Eccles Journal*.

A series of defeats followed before a 5-0 home win over fellow strugglers Walkden brought a temporary respite. "The Canal side cannot get together a combination" reported the *Eccles Journal* "and the officials made a serious mistake in playing foreign players. Both Barton and Walkden have fallen on evil days."

Barton did win 7-0 at bottom club Blackpool but defeats at Radcliffe and Altrincham saw Barton with only four points from nine games. Home attendances were now numbered in their hundreds and a South East Lancashire League game against Altrincham, on 19 November 1898, proved to be Barton's final game. A very thin crowd saw a desultory scoreless draw. Barton was due to play at Fleetwood on 26 November but notice was sent that they would not be making the journey "due to financial difficulties." A week later Ulverston did not play at Tetlow Fold as Barton refused to give a guarantee that it could fulfil the return fixture.

Officials hung on for a few weeks, seeking to find some way out of the spiralling debts, but at the last meeting before Christmas of the Lancashire Second Competition, Barton official Mr J Dean gave the solemn news that the club had disbanded.

The competition from neighbouring senior clubs, both for spectators and players, meant that Barton was always fighting a losing battle trying to keep up. Briefly the club had scaled the heights and achieved some success but financial problems were never far away as ambition exceeded resources. The implementation of broken-time was always going to be a problem for clubs such as Barton, whose gates could rarely meet the costs involved. For a time attendances had exceeded all expectations but when they reached a more natural level the problems set in.

Barton Rugby Football Club.

November 2nd, 1896.

Gentlemen,

My Committee think the time has come when the Rugby Union in London should understand our position in the North and so far as this part of the Country is concerned the policy of rigged stiff back pound of flesh policy is being adhered. We who have remained true to the Union must make our own course, particularly when there are already two Strong Northern Union Clubs playing at either side of us, which is greatly effecting our gates and taking some of our best players, unless there is an alteration in this system we shall speedily come to grief.

Two years ago they suspended a player Mr. FRANK MILES, who was found guilty of professionalism, he alone now being the Sufferer, although Club Officials who tempted him were more guilty and was in a sense ignored. We have tried quite recently to get him reinstated and it was passed by the Lancashire County Committee but the South of England Officials refused to confirm it.

We think he has more than paid the penalty and ought to be allowed to play. Had he been reinstated it would have increased our gates and those also we play against, we therefore purpose playing him and forcing this part of the County to take some action whereby we can play good players who have suffered a penalty of sufficient duration, and wish to know if you will fulfill your Matches with us, should we push the matter to an issue.

(P.S. An Early reply will oblige.)

Yours faithfully,

HY. PENNINGTON, Hon. Sec.

JOS. SCHOFIELD, Hon. Tres.

JAS. FLETCHER, Chairman.

A letter sent by Barton officials to the Lancashire County Rugby Union outlines some of the problems facing a junior club remaining loyal to the Rugby Union during the early years of the Northern Union.

Birkenhead Wanderers

FOUNDED: c 1871
CEASED: 1904
REASON: financial problems
GROUND: St Annes Enclosure
HEADQUARTERS: Queens Hotel
COLOURS: Maroon jerseys, white shorts

THE origins of the Birkenhead Wanderers club seem to be shrouded in mystery. Philip Beacall, in his book "Birkenhead Park- the first one hundred years", written in 1971 suggests that the Wanderers club was in existence prior to 1871. He wrote "Two of the clubs from which Birkenhead Park was formed, Claughton and Birkenhead Wanderers, must have been in existence before the foundation of the Rugby Union which celebrated its centenary just one year before Park..."

This indicates that Birkenhead Wanderers was in existence prior to 1870 but, sadly, the writers were unable to find any evidence of the club being active at this time. In fact, early in 1885 there is a reference to Birkenhead Park actually playing at the "St Annes Enclosure", a ground which the Wanderers used at the beginning of their existence.

Wanderers played at the St Annes Enclosure, about half-a-mile from the Park ground and as the nickname of the *Little 'Uns* implied was in the position of being a small club in close proximity to a much larger one. Strangely enough, the ground was known locally as the St Annes Enclosure but, outside the district, was always referred to as the Park Station Ground due to its location by the Park railway station.

Wanderers came to the fore with their victory in the Junior Challenge Cup of the West Lancashire Union in 1889. Forty clubs had entered the competition and Wanderers defeated Ince in the final. The committee praised the Birkenhead club "for the able manner in which they distinguished themselves."

Wanderers achieved further notable recognition in 1890-91 when invited to compete in the West Lancashire League. However, the club won only two and drew three of the 12 league games and finished sixth, behind Walkden, Aspull, Wigan, St Helens and Leigh and above Pemberton. The top clubs left the competition after this season, denying Wanderers a number of attractive fixtures.

The *Little 'Uns* were quite successful during their time in the Rugby Union and regularly took on the senior Welsh clubs as well as venturing into Lancashire and Yorkshire. Rugby was very strong on the Wirral around this time with New Brighton, Birkenhead Park, Birkenhead Wanderers and Tranmere Wanderers playing alongside smaller clubs such as Claughton and Ashford House.

In January 1896, Wanderers full-back Sam Houghton was chosen to play for England against Wales at Blackheath. Houghton had first won an international cap while playing for Runcorn in 1892. England won convincingly and Houghton was selected for the next game, against Ireland. However, he decided to rejoin his former club, now members of the Northern Union, and was rendered ineligible.

In 1896-97 Wanderers played in the Cheshire Rugby Championship alongside Altrincham, Birkenhead Park, New Brighton and Sale and, having lost only one game, finished top of the table. Despite this success, Wanderers joined the Northern Union, in all probability, because it was felt that it would never be in a position to challenge the supremacy of Birkenhead Park, which was the premier Wirral club. On the other hand Birkenhead Wanderers did have a very good chance of

Birkenhead Wanderers

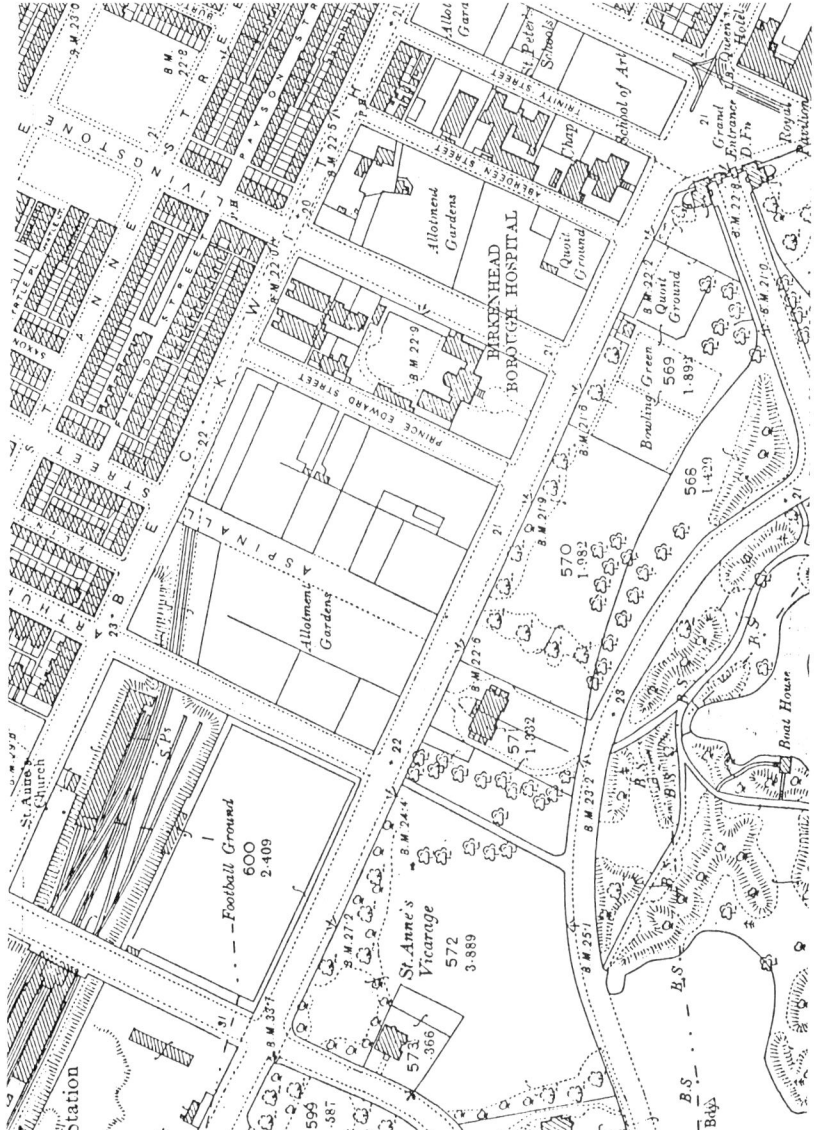

The Park Station Ground, or St. Annes Enclosure as it was known locally. The club's headquarters, The Queens Hotel, was at Birkenhead Park entrance. (Reproduced from 1897 Ordnance Survey Map)

becoming the premier Northern Union club in the Wirral. The *Birkenhead News* carried a report on the AGM of the club, held on 22 May 1897, which gives an insight into the decision made to join the Northern Union:

BIRKENHEAD WANDERERS AND THE NORTHERN UNION.

The Birkenhead Wanderers Football club, after mature consideration, has resolved to associate itself with the Northern Union. This step is one which was not altogether unexpected but the decision has, nevertheless, created a certain amount of surprise in some quarters and has given rise to a good deal of comment. The proposition was, it appears, to make application for admission to the new second division of the Lancashire Competition under the Union. An informal meeting of the players was held at the club's headquarters on Saturday evening and it was found that thirty of the players were willing to take the step. It was afterwards reported that several of the old officials are likely to resign. On Tuesday evening the annual meeting of members of the club took place in the Queens Hotel. There was a large attendance and the chair was occupied by Mr Ellis Hurst who congratulated the club on their excellent record during the past season and cordially wished them every success in the Northern Union which they had just joined. Although they had in the eyes of the Rugby Union become so-called "professionals" he assured them that the club was to be still carried on upon strictly amateur lines. The main object in going over was simply to better themselves as far as football was concerned and to do their best for local rugby football (hear). The Hon. Sec., Mr John Love, then read his report which showed that the past season had been one of the most successful in the club's history. The first team had played 30 matches, winning 21, losing 5 and drawing 4 scoring 251 points against 98...

So this was not a club struggling to get fixtures or make ends meet. This was a club which had just completed one of its best years on record and yet wanted to play Northern Union football. It was a game the Wirral public was not familiar with but appeared to be keenly interested in. The *Birkenhead Advertiser* of the time provided a fascinating insight into the Wanderers' venture. On 4 September 1897 as the new season was fast approaching the reporter wrote:-

"The new method of scoring is easy to follow. A goal however obtained counts 2 points, a try which is more difficult to score 3 points. Simple isn't it?"

He was writing after the club's first practice match played in front of 600 spectators. Wanderers' enclosure, which was owned by the council, had also been spruced up ready for the new venture as the reporter was quick to observe: "The ground is in excellent condition and the spectators' portion has been admirably banked with cinders which makes a dry footing and allows for everyone witnessing the game easily...." Wanderers' first competitive game in the Northern Union was away to Swinton on 4 September 1897, a friendly match which saw the club lose 0-25. However, Birkenhead was far from down-hearted for it had played a senior club of some standing. The first home game was against old Rugby Union rival Altrincham on the following Saturday and the Little 'Uns produced a 10-0 victory much to the delight of a large crowd. The reporter would have us believe that the crowd considered the game to be an improvement on the Rugby Union fare they had been watching for many years:

"There was a large crowd....the majority, however, are fully of the opinion that a decided improvement had been made in the game...."

What was even more interesting was the comments he made regarding the style of play adopted by the Altrincham team. "Altrincham have acquired the trick of never being tackled with the ball. On being held they drop the ball. This was noticeable. The more loose the ball is kept the more open the play. The more open the play the more chances are offered for scoring...."

One other amazing fact which came to light was the revelation that the club's next home game, against Walkden on 18 September, was actually filmed by a Mr Coates who apparently used to film local events and then show them at the local YMCA. The players, however, appear to have been just as "hammy" then as they are now for the reporter again wrote "When the players saw the cinematograph man at work it was funny to notice how the play was kept at the side nearest to the machine!"

It is extremely unlikely that this film remains in existence but it would have afforded a unique opportunity to observe Rugby League being played in its earliest days. This is, perhaps, the earliest recorded evidence of a rugby match being filmed.

Wanderers got off to a fine start losing only one of the first six matches. Obviously the form of the previous season had been maintained even though the club had switched codes. Thereafter a decline set in and Wanderers eventually finished in seventh position. One amusing incident occurred during the season and involved one of the club's best players. The local reporter wrote: "On Saturday, whilst playing for Birkenhead Wanderers against Fleetwood, Frank Ingham had a couple of teeth knocked out and one day this week he received a mysterious looking parcel in the shape of a box used in jewellery. On being opened, however, the "jewellery" was found to consist of a couple of enormous teeth and a long hair snugly ensconced in a bed of cotton wool. Whether the teeth were meant to replace those displaced it was best left to the lively imagination of my readers but I may mention that they are big enough to fit a good sized horse......truly someone had a pretty wit..."

The club's fortunes in the second season remained very much unchanged and it again finished seventh as Wanderers took time to adjust to the faster, more free-flowing Northern Union game. In 1899-1900 progress was made and Wanderers eventually finished in fourth spot with nine wins and two draws in 19 games.

In 1900-01 Wanderers enjoyed its best season in the Second Competition, due largely to the acquisition of a former Welsh Rugby Union international forward, Tom Pook. Having originally joined the Northern Union code with Holbeck the former Newport player came to reside in the town and brought with him a talented winger called Llewellyn. Pook acted as unofficial coach and hired electrical Wells lights so that the players could train in the evenings. Though nearing the end of his career Pook made a tremendous impact, on and off the field, during his short stay at Birkenhead.

Having traditionally relied on local players, the club recruited a number of other outsiders including a talented half-back, Edmunds, from Heckmondwike, and another Welshman, Ringwall, from Wigan. Wanderers won nine of the opening ten league games and looked set for the championship. Home crowds, which had shown signs of falling-off, rose to around the three thousand mark. Inexplicably, Wanderers needing only one win in the last three games to make sure of the title, lost them all. The team went down 2-6 to eventual champions Morecambe and, over a disastrous Easter programme, lost 2-9 to Tyldesley and 0-2 to Werneth.

In the event Wanderers did achieve its long awaited ambition of senior status in 1901-02. Broughton Rangers, Salford, Swinton, Runcorn, Warrington, Oldham and Leigh left the Lancashire Senior Competition to form a new Northern League together with seven clubs from Yorkshire. Wanderers, Lancaster, Morecambe, Altrincham and Radcliffe from the now-defunct Second Competition and Hull KR filled the vacant places. Wanderers finished ninth though only one of its eight wins, against Stockport, was against a club which had enjoyed senior status the previous season.

A new Northern League competition was established in 1902-03, with two divisions, each comprising 18 clubs. Wanderers finished ninth in the Second Division a most satisfac-

Former Welsh Rugby Union International Tom Pook made a tremendous impact at Birkenhead. (Photograph courtesy Robert Gate)

Birkenhead Wanderers

tory situation considering that, geographically, it was out on a limb and had to finance trips to South Shields, Dewsbury, Leeds and Keighley to name but a few. The shortest journeys were to Rochdale Hornets and Stockport and the problem was that few of the Yorkshire sides Birkenhead now faced regularly were considered attractive opposition. Home crowds fell to such low numbers that the club was not even covering its expenses. Wanderers had to sell some of its best players to survive and a young half-back, Fred Gleave, joined Wigan to which he gave a long and distinguished service.

It was looking ominous for the club but the fighting spirit of the committee took it into the 1903-04 season. The Wanderers tag was dropped and it was decided to leave the St Annes Enclosure and share Prenton Park with Tranmere Rovers association club. Rovers went on to achieve Football League status in 1921, moved ground in 1912 and the new home was also called Prenton Park. The original ground is now referred to as Old Prenton Park.

Ground-sharing had its problems, with Rovers having precedence if home fixtures clashed so the rugby club had to play some games at the Docks Station enclosure, owned by the Wirral Railway Company. The finances of the club were now in such a crippled state that the Birkenhead committee decided to stage two mid week home games during January, against Holbeck and Wakefield Trinity, at Wigan. The club was rewarded with higher gates than might have been expected but the move served to alienate the few remaining loyal followers. For a number of away games Birkenhead was unable to raise a full complement of players and, for the long trip to South Shields in April, played three short and not surprisingly was hammered 0-42. It was something of an achievement in itself to avoid the wooden spoon as Birkenhead finished fourth from bottom, with seven league wins, all of them at home.

Birkenhead began the 1904-05 season with the finances of the club at breaking point. "All the players worth a place in a good team have gone to where the grass grows greenest" reported the *Birkenhead News*. A side containing several junior players from the Runcorn area travelled to Brighouse on the opening day of the season, 3 September, and came away with a 0-31 hiding. The following Saturday, Birkenhead played what was, unwittingly, to be the last match at home losing 0-25 to York. The gate was insufficient to cover the cost of staging the match. The following week Birkenhead travelled up to Lancaster and was again defeated 0-14. It was then that the gods conspired to break the club and sent Birkenhead into oblivion.

Birkenhead should have had a home match against Holbeck but the Yorkshire club had defected to the fast-growing game of soccer (Holbeck was eventually to become the Leeds United of today). This deprived Birkenhead of a home game and the opportunity to gain some much needed revenue which would have enabled the side to fulfil the next fixture. The story of what then happened is much better told through the words of the reporter of the day:

SATURDAY 1 OCTOBER 1904: *"Birkenhead were left without a match last Saturday owing to Holbeck's conversion to the soccer code."*

WEDNESDAY 5 OCTOBER 1904: *"The Wanderers, for the club is still in conversation given its old but now unofficial title, are in trouble.....the next step lies with the Northern Union....a suggestion has been made that the club should turn to soccer, no doubt with the hope of paying off some of the financial responsibilities incurred...it is pretty certain that Northern Unionism is dead in Birkenhead....but the real mistake was made years ago when they joined the Northern Union, in which their geographical position was an extreme one, becoming worse with the decline of other clubs in the county. Their income has not been commensurate with their heavy travelling expenses, that in short, has lead up to the present crisis..."*

SATURDAY 8 OCTOBER 1904: "The announcement on Saturday that the committee of the Birkenhead club has decided not to fulfil their match with Pontefract, owing to financial difficulties, did not come as great surprise to the local football public. But the news aroused feeling of regret and sympathy amongst those who remember the palmy days of the old Wanderers.... The club was poorly supported in the only home game in September with York and which did not pay expenses, I believe....and the defection of Holbeck, which deprived them of a home match on Saturday week, accelerated the crisis for the club had then to play two away matches in succession."

SATURDAY 15 OCTOBER 1904: "The plucky efforts of the committee to prolong the life of the Birkenhead club have come to nought. They fulfilled the league fixture with Dewsbury on Saturday (8 October) but found it beyond their resources to make another long and expensive journey to Barrow today. In these circumstances no other course remained but to resign from the League and at a meeting of the league committee at Huddersfield on Tuesday evening (11 October) the resignation was accepted. Conditions were imposed by the league committee with a view to obviating any loss to York, the only club to visit Birkenhead.... with regard to the Dewsbury match, the side made a good fight with their unbeaten opponents in the first half but failed to last. I may state what I refrained from doing last week in view of the club's precarious position and that is that the committee are to blame for deciding to visit a smallpox infested area quite unnecessarily as their subsequent resignation has proved. What great difference was there between bringing the Dewsbury team to Birkenhead and sending their own team there, I fail to see, for the chance of creating another smallpox outbreak here is fairly equal by either course...

The officials are going to carry on the club, so Mr Love informs me, by the arrangement of friendly fixtures as far as possible..."

A club which had battled bravely to keep the Northern Union flag flying on the Wirral and was intent on continuing the fight was eventually downed by circumstances over which it had no control. The defection of the Holbeck club to association football, coupled with an outbreak of smallpox in Dewsbury, conspired to rob Birkenhead of two vital home matches and possible revenue which might have seen the club through a difficult financial period. The result was that the club was unable to raise the necessary finance to travel to Pontefract and Barrow and, sadly, Birkenhead ceased to exist within the Northern Union.

Once lost, the game of Northern Union or, as it became Rugby League, never returned to the area.

Blackpool

FOUNDED: 1898
CEASED: 1899
REASON: financial problems
GROUND: Raikes Hall Gardens
HEADQUARTERS: Adelphi Hotel
COLOURS: White jerseys, blue shorts

THE Blackpool club had a meteoric rise after first seeing the light of day towards the end of the 1897-98 season when a group of local sportsmen decided that the handling code, which had been played up the coast at Fleetwood, offered them the chance of some sport and recreation.

The first recorded match in which the club was involved was a friendly game played to raise money for the widow of a Mr Richard Simpson of Fleetwood. This match was played on 19 February 1898 at the Copse Ground against Fleetwood. Blackpool was represented by: Knight; Firth, Dyson, W Turner, Dennis; Jones, Yeadon; J Turner, Hilton, H Ward, R Turner, Maxwell, Clarke, Dunne, Inman and Langman. The Blackpool team, in an attempt to even up the match, was allowed to play with an extra forward.

This match highlighted the intense rivalry which existed between the two resorts. It proved to be the match which was instrumental in establishing a second Northern Union professional club on the Fylde Coast. The Blackpool club moved swiftly to capitalise on this new found enthusiasm. As the reporter on the *Fleetwood Express* wrote on 9 March: "....following up the venture made at Fleetwood a few weeks ago a number of locals have interested themselves in rugby football and practice matches have been entered into at Raikes Hall....."

The local Blackpool paper a day earlier had carried a more informative reference: "Several of our local athletes have talked the question over as to the advisability of forming a club under the rugby football amateur rules and a great interest was manifested in the movement....A meeting of all local athletes and other interested in the movement is to be held at the Adelphi Hotel on Church Road at 8 o'clock tonight....as late as the season is matches can be arranged at home, to Owen's College and Fleetwood, in order to let Blackpudlians see if they find the new organisation worth supporting...."

The support was obviously there for a second meeting was held, again in the Adelphi Hotel, on Friday 11 March 1898, when the club officially came into being. Mr WR Hooper of Elswick was elected president with Mr J Yates the secretary. The club's headquarters was to be the Adelphi Hotel and the ground was to be at Raikes Hall Gardens in the centre of town. At this meeting the club decided to apply for membership of the Lancashire Second Competition of the Northern Union. If Fleetwood was in the second division then Blackpool would have to be also.

Blackpool was successful in its application and set about preparing for the coming season with a vengeance. Friendly games were arranged to assess players' abilities and to help it sign new players. The first of these matches was played on 19 March 1898, against those players from Fleetwood who worked at the Alkali Works and who named themselves Thornton Rangers. The fledgling club gained its first victory 6-0.

The available evidence suggests that the club was officially unveiled to the paying public of Blackpool with typical razzamatazz on Good Friday 8 April 1898. The club rather ambitiously arranged two matches. The second team played Broughton Rangers second team in the morning, losing 11-34, and with

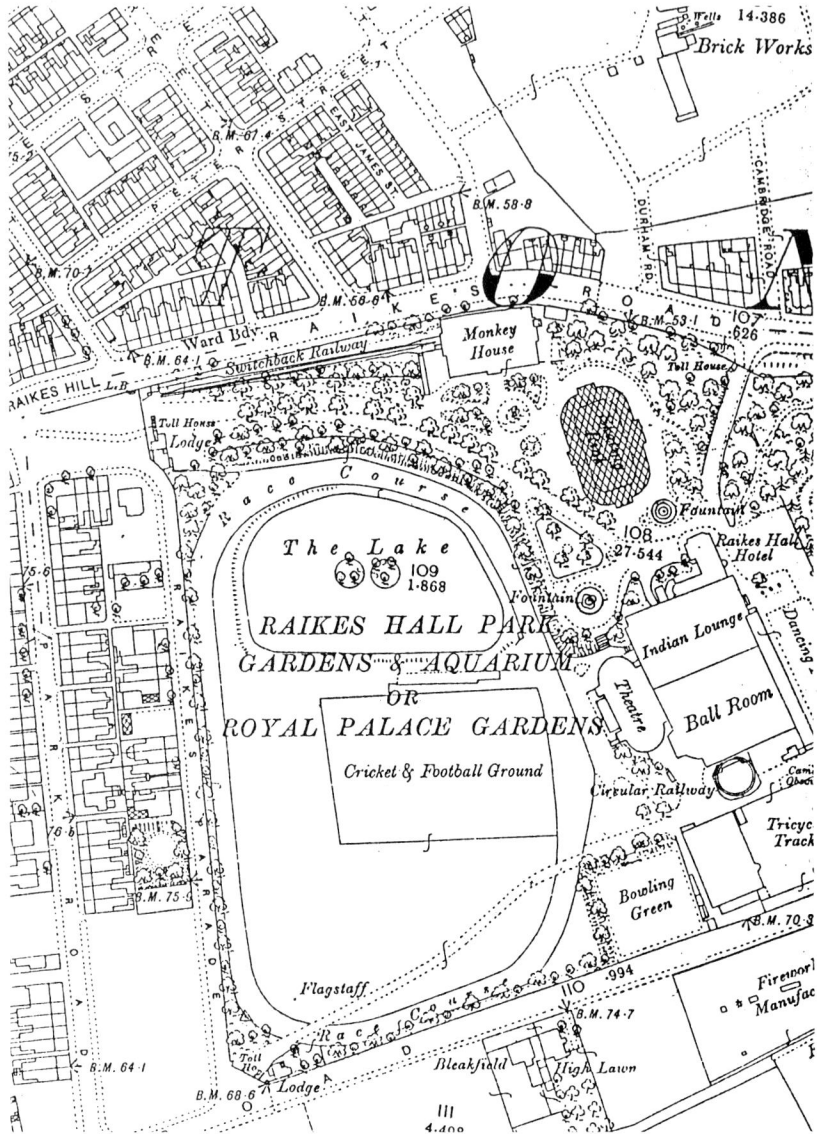

The Raikes Hall Gardens with the football ground. The Raikes Hall Hotel is still there along with the bowling green. (Reproduced from 1893 Ordnance Survey Map)

this game out of the way the first team game was kicked-off by the mayor of Blackpool, Mr Robert Butcher Mather. The opposition was Swinton Parish Church which won 6-2. The mayor then joined the players and officials "....about 60 in number who enjoyed a knife and fork tea in the small ballroom...."

Given a rousing send-off by the town officials, Blackpool played one more friendly game going down 0-18 to a strong Huddersfield second team. That game completed Blackpool settled down to prepare for the demands of the second division.

The 1898-99 season began for Blackpool on the first official day of the season, 1 September. Blackpool's first league game was at Birkenhead Wanderers, a daunting one for a fledgling club but especially so as the game was staged on a Thursday evening and many players were unable to leave work in time. The home side won 24-0 but the newcomers were praised for their plucky display.

Two days later home fixtures opened with a visit from Altrincham in front of 300 spectators, most of them supporting the visitors. Altrincham proved to be too strong and experienced and won 19-3. The following Saturday, Millom travelled to Raikes Hall and handed out a 52-0 drubbing to the *Seasiders*.

The scene was now set for the first clash between two professional clubs on the Fylde Coast when, only three weeks into the season, Fleetwood was due at Raikes Hall. The teams that day, Saturday 17 September 1898, were:

BLACKPOOL - Knight; Jobson, Anderton, Appleton, Scott; Wedgewood, Travers; Gill, Carson, Rollins, Parr, Swinton, Blakely, Midgley, Little.

FLEETWOOD - Dennett; Mitchinson, Harrison, Dempsey, Evans; Foster, Hayes; Catterall, Benson, Walsh, Roche, McNicolas, Kay, Brooks, Little.

Fleetwood, with tries by Hayes, Evans, Foster, Roche and Benson and goals from Benson and Mitchinson, won 19-5. Anderton, whose displays in a struggling side often won praise, scored Blackpool's points, with a try and a goal.

The clubs met four times in the league that season, twice in the Second Competition and twice in the new South East Lancashire League (SELL), which had been set up in an attempt to create some local interest. It was not a success and was dropped at the end of the season. It was in a SELL match that Blackpool managed a 3-0 victory.

Blackpool was rooted to the bottom of the

A photograph of the Blackpool club in action in 1898, probably against local rivals Fleetwood.

Second Competition and suffered some heavy defeats the worst being 3-57 to Barrow and 0-67 to Millom. Blackpool was also struggling off the field and the lack of success caused the directors at Raikes Hall to withdraw their support forcing Blackpool to move and play the rest of the matches at the athletics track in Whitegate Lane. It was, however, in January 1899 that the local paper first reported the signs of impending demise:

"...Blackpool should have played Altrincham in a South East Lancashire League match...the match was cancelled with Blackpool having withdrawn from the SELL..the public seem to be of the opinion that the club is finished...there is a certain amount of hope that the club will continue to exist..."

The club did manage to struggle on until April when, ironically, it was Fleetwood which was to knock the final nail into the club's coffin. Blackpool and Fleetwood were drawn together in the qualifying round of the Challenge Cup with the winner travelling to Widnes in the first round. As the Fleetwood reporter stated: "The prospects of a share of the gate at Widnes, perhaps £50 or £60, would halve the club's debts."

The Blackpool scribe was also aware of the problems facing both clubs: "The contestants were as keen as the edge of a newly set razor, for the result of the match meant more than the honour of going into the first round, it meant half the gate at Widnes which may be anything from £40 to £60, an amount calculated to set either club on their financial legs."

Fleetwood ran out winners 13-6 and the tie virtually spelled the end for Blackpool, no £60, no reduction in the club's debts and, finally, no club. Blackpool struggled on for a few weeks and played its final league game at home to Radcliffe on 1 April 1899, ironically giving one of the best displays of the season, losing only 2-6.

The league table told its own story. Blackpool played 16 games and lost them all scoring 31 points and conceding 415. A further two matches were played, at home to Barton and away to Walkden, which were later expunged when those two clubs disbanded during the season. Blackpool lost these matches too, 0-7 and 0-13.

Blackpool attempted to solve its problems by amalgamating with the local football club. On 4 April it was reported: "It may be when the South Shore association and the Blackpool Rugby Clubs join together that the latter team may improve..." The results of these negotiations were never publicly revealed, but it can be assumed that they failed, although South Shore did amalgamate with another association club to form Blackpool AFC. After playing just one more game, a friendly against Pendlebury on 8 April 1899, losing 0-3, Blackpool went out of existence.

The Blackpool club had been going for only 14 months. There were many reasons for its failure. The team entered the Northern Union at a time when professionalism had been introduced, thus reducing the number of players willing to travel to play for clubs such as Blackpool. The players were not winning matches and so failed to capture the imagination of the paying public. Pride also played a part, it might have been advantageous for Blackpool to start at a local level and play in one of the Lancashire junior leagues in which it would have played opposition comparable in ability.

Crompton

FOUNDED: 1884
CEASED: 1898
REASON: financial difficulties
GROUND: Rushcroft
HEADQUARTERS: Woolpack Inn, Shaw
COLOURS: Navy blue

FORMED in 1884, Crompton played at the Rushcroft ground, situated to the north of the village of Shaw in the foothills of the Pennines. Crompton had to function in the shadow of Oldham but, like fellow junior club Werneth, did so quite effectively until the Northern Union came along.

Elected to membership of the Lancashire County Rugby Union on 1 November 1887, Crompton was invited to join the Lancashire Club Championship (Third Class) in the 1894-95 season and completed a highly satisfactory campaign, finishing as runners-up to champions Pemberton. The number of clubs joining the Northern Union was such that in the following season Crompton found itself elevated to the first-class ranks and, with 17 points from 20 games, finished in mid-table.

Before the season was out, Crompton decided to resign from the Rugby Union and played its first game under the Northern Union, losing 3-4 to St Helens Recs on 25 April 1896. The Crompton side on this occasion was: Wilde; Whitworth, Smethurst, Riley, Butley; Harwood, Harrop; Butterworth, Boardman, Kay, Whitehead, Stockton, Harrison, Hetherington, Gibson.

"Undoubtedly something had to be done....to rescue these clubs from oblivion" outlined one match report. "Spectators do not want to see friendly games...and the clubs are merely trying to safeguard their own futures."

The 1896-97 season was something of a disappointment for clubs such as Crompton which had joined the Northern Union in their droves. Although rumours abounded about the formation of a Second Competition it was not until the end of the season that this finally came to fruition. Some of the impetus was lost as breakaway clubs, excluded from the senior ranks, filled in time with a whole series of friendly games, often playing the same opponents three or four times.

Crompton's only competitive matches were in the newly-formed Challenge Cup competition but the performance, after a first round bye and second round win over Bradford Churchill, did not augur well. Crompton was humbled at Halifax, in the third round, conceding fifty points without reply.

Even so Crompton took its appointed place in the Second Competition with hopes of a successful season ahead. The prospects, however, were overshadowed by a debt of around £150 which had accrued simply through paying broken-time in the previous season.

"It is hoped to clear off the debt with the aid of a bazaar to be held in December" was the optimistic tone reported in the *Rochdale Observer*." The travel costs will be heavy and good gates are needed to enable the club to keep its head above water" was the more realistic tone reflected by the *Oldham Chronicle*. As an economy measure it was decided to disband the A team.

Crompton had the distinction of providing the first opposition under Northern Union rules for Hull KR, travelling across to the east coast on the season's opening day, 4 September 1897. The home side romped to a 31-0 victory. Two days later a crowd of 5000 saw Oldham beat Crompton 12-0 in a benefit game.

Crompton began life in the Second Competition on 11 September 1897 with Knott, Har-

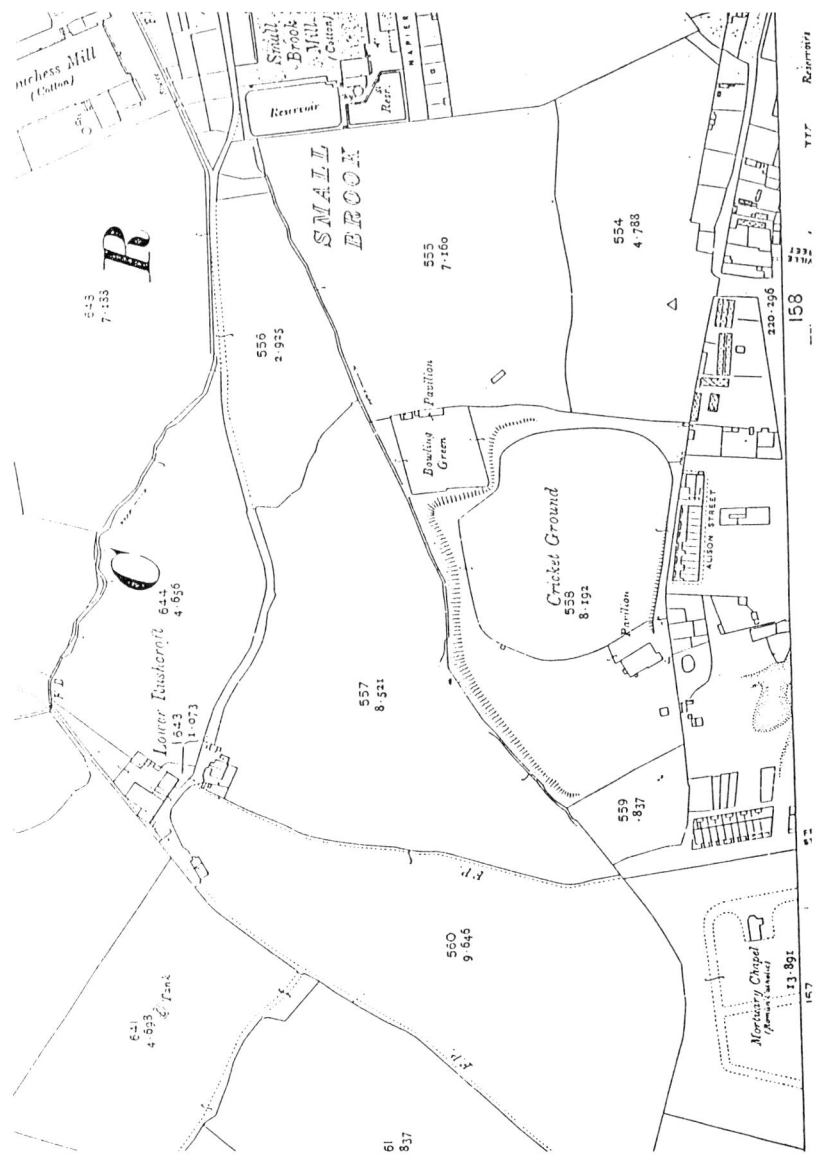

Crompton shared its ground at Rushcroft with the cricket club. (Reproduced from the 1893 Ordnance Survey Map)

wood and Dunkerley scoring tries in a 9-0 win at Fleetwood. Harry Knott, signed from Oldham, was regarded as a fine acquisition and appointed captain.

Defeats at Walkden and Radcliffe followed but in the first home game Crompton handed out an 8-2 defeat to big spenders Barton with Knott and Midgley scoring tries in a thrilling contest. Despite this a "poor" crowd saw Crompton's next home game, a 3-7 defeat at the hands of Altrincham. "The gates are unworthy of a district which contains so many football followers" concluded the *Oldham Chronicle*.

To make matters worse, Crompton's home game with Radcliffe had to be postponed after the authorities shut the ground for a period of two weeks "due to repeated disorderly conduct by spectators." The punishment could have been worse but for the intervention of the Wesleyan minister at Shaw, Rev Josiah Evans, who wrote in defence of the club.

Defeats at Barton and St Helens Recs followed and for the visit of Birkenhead Wanderers only a few hundred were in attendance at the Rushcroft ground. The financial situation was clearly worsening and some of the players signed at the start of the season were now conspicuous by their absence.

In the last home game before Christmas only a hundred spectators were present for a local derby against Werneth. Crompton should have played against Birkenhead Wanderers over Christmas but had to scratch the fixture due to an inability to raise a side. To answer the growing rumours of financial crisis the committee organised a meeting of creditors at the club's headquarters, the Woolpack Inn, Shaw, on 29 December 1897.

The debt, it was reported, had now risen to £300 and an offer to pay the creditors 10 shillings in the pound was accepted. "At one time the financial position was such that the creditors did not expect a farthing" reported the *Rochdale Observer* "and the club will continue as normal."

For the visit to Altrincham, on New Year's Day, a weakened Crompton side was in evidence and the hosts ran in 23 points without reply. Crompton's side was largely made up of players from local junior clubs with only Greenwood, Whitworth, Harwood and Durham remaining from the first team which had started the season.

"These are evil days" decided the *Rochdale Observer* "as many of the players have deserted the club in its hour of need." An appeal was broadcast for a good crowd for the next home game, against Fleetwood, but only a smattering of spectators witnessed a hard-fought win against the competition's bottom club.

Crompton made an appeal to Oldham for funds being aware that earlier in the season Swinton had given Walkden £20 to enable them to continue. Oldham appeared to decline but Rochdale Hornets did step in with the offer of a friendly on half gate terms. A crowd of 1500 saw Crompton go down 0-35 at Dane Street but this was to be only a temporary financial respite.

"Only with the greatest difficulty" did Crompton raise a side to entertain Millom on 29 January and the visitors ran out easy winners 24-2. Though a scratch side had done its best the *Oldham Chronicle* reporter had clearly had enough. "It is disgusting to watch such exhibitions every week" he wrote.

A meeting of the committee was held on Monday 31 January 1898 and, by a majority, it was decided to disband the club. This decision was put to the members at a Special Meeting held at the Woolpack two days later and the motion to disband was carried with few dissenters.

Crompton became the first Second Competition club to fold during a season but it was not the last. A few weeks later the competition was thrown into turmoil and the league table again re-calculated when St Helens Recs called it a day and the following season saw both Barton and Walkden close down.

The costs of travel and wages for broken-time had been the most important factors in

Crompton's demise. In joining the Northern Union the club had acted in its own self-interest and would have been left with precious few opponents to play against had it remained in the Rugby Union. Yet with little assistance forthcoming from the senior clubs, or any direction or financial aid from the authorities, clubs such as Crompton which a few years previously had appeared in a healthy state had a one-way ticket to oblivion.

Dalton

FOUNDED: 1885
CEASED: 1900
REASON: reverted to amateur ranks
GROUND: Railway Meadow
HEADQUARTERS: Railway Hotel
COLOURS: Red and black

DALTON'S rise into the ranks of the Lancashire Second Competition was a rapid one but its stay in such company was to be brief.

A number of clubs in the town, Dalton White Rose, Lillywhites and White Star held a meeting at the Railway Hotel in 1884 with a view to amalgamating but no firm decision was made. A Dalton rugby club was formed a year later and was strengthened in 1890 when the junior clubs joined.

Since the recent county reorganisation Dalton-in-Furness is now part of Cumbria but in the 1890's was an urban district of Lancashire, situated three to four miles north-east of Barrow, on the LMS railway. There were numerous iron ore mines in the surrounding district.

Briefly elevated to senior status in the Rugby Union North-Western League in 1892-93 Dalton endured a disastrous campaign losing all 16 league games against Lancaster, Millom, Morecambe, Barrow, Kendal Hornets, Ulverston, Kendal and Askam. The following season Dalton was back in the junior ranks.

The Dalton club made its first entry in the Northern Union Challenge Cup in the 1897-98 season losing 3-13 to Barrow. At this time, the club competed in the North-West Junior League alongside Roose, Askam and Carnforth and the reserve teams of Barrow, Millom, Morecambe and Lancaster.

In 1898-99 Dalton was again elected to join the ranks of the senior clubs which competed in the North-Western League. Dalton's prestige increased considerably as a result and this time it enjoyed a satisfactory season finishing fourth behind the champions, Millom, Barrow and Workington, but in front of Maryport, Ulverston, Lancaster and Askam.

There were gaps to be filled in the Lancashire Second Competition as a result of the demise of Walkden and Barton. At the AGM Dalton was elected to membership alongside other new clubs in Whitworth and Werneth.

Barrow provided the opposition for Dalton's first match on 30 September 1899 when Dalton was represented by the following team: Lancaster; Turner, Davis, Platts, Crossley; Wilson, Saunders; Bromley, Wollard, Hetherington, Clague, Massicks, Toothill, Coulthard, Kelly. Unlike other clubs in the competition Dalton relied upon local players for its side. Barrow won 11-0 in front of a crowd

A Baines card from the 1890's featuring Dalton. (Courtesy Robert Gate)

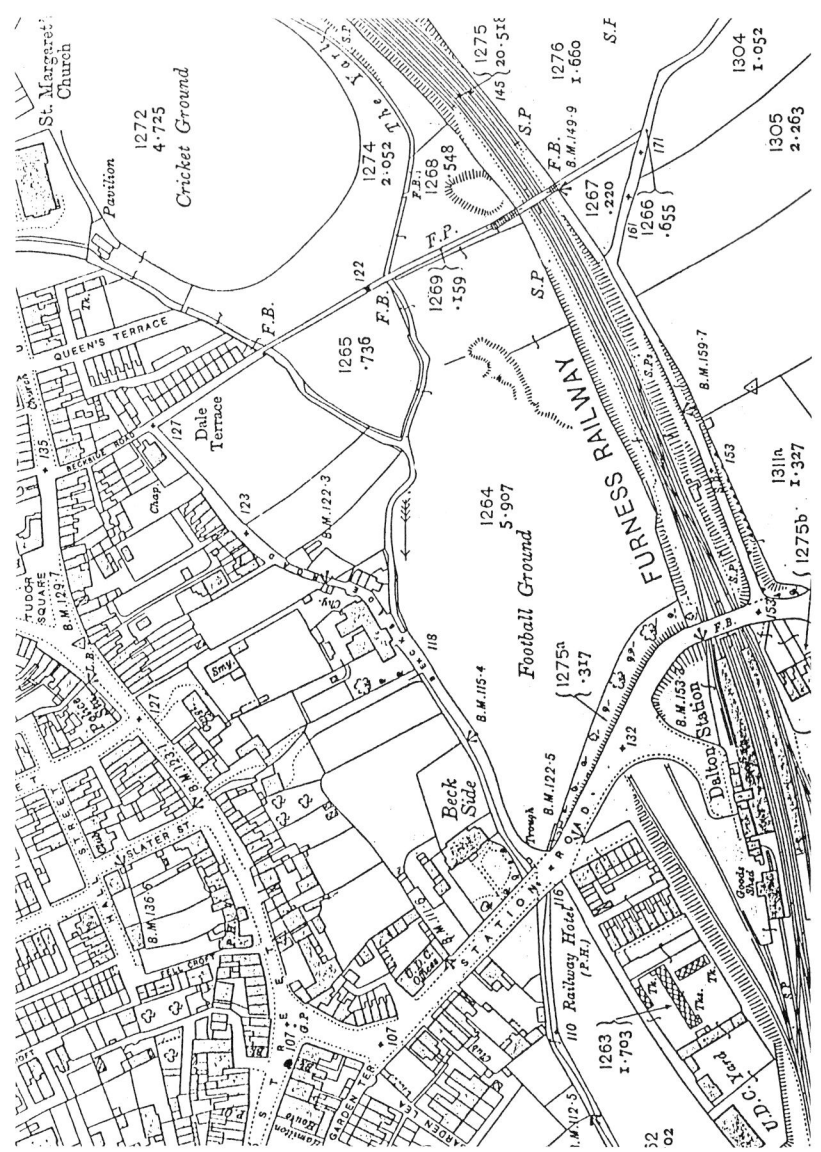

The Dalton ground at Railway Meadow. (Reproduced from 1913 Ordnance Survey Map)

described as being one of the largest ever seen at Railway Meadow.

Dalton recorded the first win at home over Fleetwood, the following Saturday, a try by Saunders proving decisive; and then lost by only a single try to neighbours Ulverston.

The opening matches had been full of encouragement but the testing time came when Dalton had to play the long distance away games. Funds for broken-time were hardly plentiful and early starts were needed to get to the south Lancashire and Cheshire grounds on time.

Dalton held its own in home games and recorded two more victories. Tries by Kelly and Massicks helped Dalton to a celebrated 10-8 win over Lancaster on a snow-covered ground. Baxter and Smith scored tries in an 8-3 win against Altrincham. A home draw was also secured against Morecambe, a fine result considering the opposition had been a first division side the previous season.

It was away from home that Dalton had problems and every game on foreign soil was lost, some by large margins, the heaviest 0-26 to Barrow. "The long train journeys have not been conducive to good form for football" concluded the local correspondent, an excuse which could presumably not be proffered in this case.

As with Ulverston the Dalton committee asked its players to accept reduced terms as the costs of competing in the Second Competition began to spiral. It was said that the club was only kept going when three players were sold to Rochdale Hornets for the sum of £25.

"The unsatisfactory monetary condition of the majority of Lancashire Second Division clubs is getting serious" alerted The Athletic News in February 1900 but there was precious little support, either financial or otherwise, from the Northern Union despite a claim for assistance from a delegation which included Dalton's representative.

This unsympathetic view was reflected by the Yorkshire Post reporter who had strong views on the subject. "Any help would have been slight and of temporary value" he stated. "Many junior clubs are experiencing the aftermath of overwhelming ambition....if a more healthy state of affairs follows, the disbandment of some of the bankrupt clubs need not be regretted."

Dalton was rooted to the foot of the table and fell behind with its fixtures, fulfilling only 16 of the 20 games. Dalton failed to play Radcliffe at all and did not travel to Fleetwood or Altrincham.

Organisational skills do not appear to been particularly high as Dalton was due to play at Fleetwood on Easter Monday but, having got to Barrow, discovered that the boat was not sailing. By then it was too late to make the journey by train. Altrincham successfully applied for compensation after Dalton's failure to travel to Devisdale due to lack of funds.

Dalton's final game in the Lancashire Second Competition resulted in a 0-9 home defeat by Werneth on 25 April. "We are wooden spoonists and no mistake" concluded the local reporter. Despite this three Dalton players, Kelly, Wollard and Coulthard were selected for the Rest of the League side which played the champions Barrow.

The financial problems meant that Dalton had to abandon a professional team after only one season. The following season, 1900-01, saw Dalton competing in the North-West Junior League alongside Ulverston. At the end of that first campaign back in the amateur ranks the club's financial state was described as being "much improved" and prospects of the game continuing in the town were now altogether brighter.

Thankfully, despite Dalton's ill-starred flirtation with professionalism, the club recovered sufficiently to be able to keep going and the rugby game was not lost to the town despite the demise of the professional team.

Fleetwood

FOUNDED: 1897
CEASED: 1901
REASON: financial problems
GROUND: Copse Ground
HEADQUARTERS: Crown Hotel
COLOURS: Red jerseys with white sash, blue shorts

RUGBY came to the Fylde coast soon after the breakaway and was probably introduced by the influx of workers from Widnes to the Fleetwood Alkali Works, which was based in Thornton. The Alkali Works later became part of the giant ICI complex.

Rugby had been played briefly at both Blackpool and Fleetwood in the past. In the 1878-79 season a cup competition was promoted at Raikes Hall, Blackpool between eight teams. Chorley eventually won the cup defeating Rossendale in the final in front of 2000 spectators. In September 1887 the Rugby Union attempted to introduce the game to the area by organising a number of exhibition matches. Rochdale Hornets played Oldham and Leeds Parish Church took on Batley over the Bank Holiday weekend at Raikes Hall. A week later, at the Copse Ground in Fleetwood, St Helens played Kendal Hornets. There is even a reference to two local teams, the Cockle Hall Rangers and the Bourne Hall Turnip Loupers, playing a game on 3 September 1887. The ventures were not successful and it was not until 1897 that rugby reappeared on the coast on a regular basis.

The first recorded Northern Union match was reported in the *Fleetwood Express* of 6 May 1897 between two teams calling themselves Thornton and Fleetwood. The match report does mention a previous game, but this was not reported in the press.

This encounter was instrumental in establishing the first regular rugby club on the Fylde Coast, based at Fleetwood. The reason why the club was set up in Fleetwood, rather than Thornton, was probably because the former was a centre with a larger population and more able to support a professional outfit. There is intriguing evidence to suggest another reason, that the Fleetwood club was formed under the auspices of the Fleetwood Rangers Football Club which was the premier semi-professional soccer club in the district. Most certainly the report of the first match in the paper suggests a strong connection between the two organisations.

If this were the case then it could be argued that Fleetwood was the first rugby club to be set up under the auspices of an association club.

A feather in the cap of the Fleetwood club was that it was the first to be formed specifically to play Northern Union football which did not have any roots in the old Rugby Union tradition. The vast majority of clubs which played in the Northern Union had been in existence prior to the initial split in 1895. It could be said that Castleford was formed before Fleetwood, specifically to play Northern Union, but Castleford arose from a split in the ranks of the local Rugby Union club at its AGM in 1896 with some members staying loyal to the Rugby Union and others forming a new Northern Union club.

The club's first official AGM was held on 29 July 1897 in the Free Library in Fleetwood. At this meeting officials were elected, a headquarters, the Crown Hotel on Dock Street officially adopted, and the club colours decided upon. It was confirmed that the club was to share the Fleetwood Rangers Copse Road Ground. Fleetwood, through its first captain Mr D Bowen Evans, a Welshman who had been signed from Wigan, became a founder member of the Second Competition.

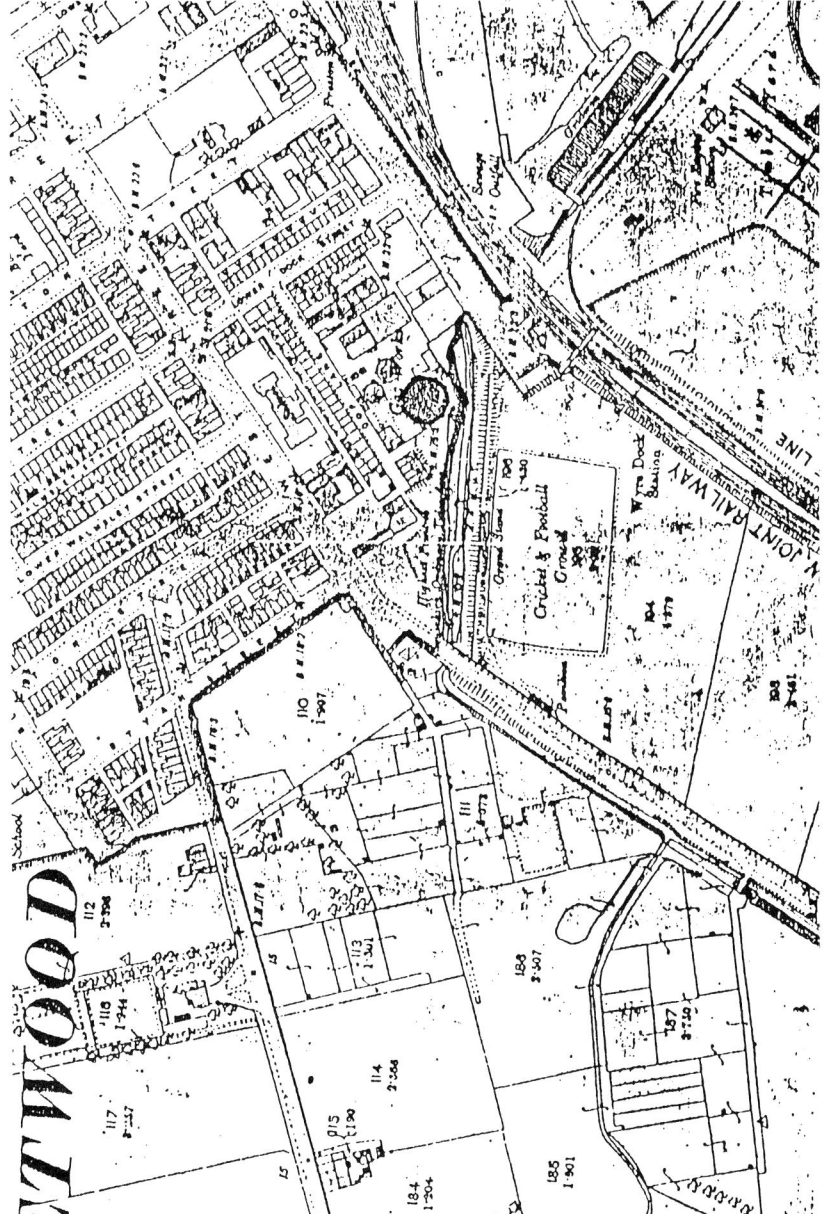

The Copse Ground. West Street is now Lord Street. (Reproduced from 1891 Ordnance Survey Map)

The club had many problems to surmount before it played its first league game. The local Fleetwood newspaper gave a good insight into these: "....New players have been signed....Robinson (formerly of Wigan) at three-quarter....Harrison a forward of Wigan....a first class half-back has been found in Dr Rhodes (of Owen's College)....Hayes a half-back from Tyldesley (Buff Berry's partner)....Tittle (Stockport) and Ross (Runcorn)...."

The club was still awaiting the arrival of its playing strip: "so far the players have not had a dress rehearsal, as the costumes are not ready, but Mr Jas Read of East Street (now Lord Street) has the contract in hand."

The playing strip was ready for the first match against Lancaster at Quay Meadow on Saturday 4 September 1897. Fleetwood was not expected to win as the Lancaster players were "old warhorses" of rugby, but it was a game in which the club really needed to produce a good performance if it were to be taken seriously by the Fleetwood public. Fleetwood lost 5-14 but was not disgraced. The Fleetwood team that day was:

Aughton; Knowles, B Evans, Young, Kight; Hayes, Hague; Henderson, Lanigan, Faulkner, S Evans, Gibson, Dutton, Millington, Dempsey.

Hayes had the honour of scoring Fleetwood's first try and Knowles kicked a goal.

There were many administrative difficulties to be overcome in a fledgling club and the travel arrangements came into question as the local reporter stated. "A sixteen mile drive by wagonettes, on such an afternoon as Saturday's, was not conducive to the playing of good football and though song and lively conversation made the time pass rapidly the stiffness was there all the same...."

Although Fleetwood did not get off to the anticipated start, hopes were high that the first home match would see the defeat of a Crompton side, thought to be one of the weakest in the competition. An unchanged Fleetwood team took the field and left it with a 0-9 defeat. It was a losing habit that would have to wait until the following February to be broken. The players were destined to win only one league match in their first season, 8-0 at home to Barton. They did win friendly matches against the likes of Dalton, Blackpool and Whitworth but the crowds were looking for league wins and so support dwindled.

It was the new Challenge Cup competition which was to see the new club have some success. In the first round it beat Warrington St Mary's, a Third Competition outfit, 6-3. The following Saturday Fleetwood undertook a four hour train journey and defeated Lostock Gralam 10-0 to earn a home tie against Hull KR at the Copse Ground. This had all the makings of a real "needle" match as the two ports were rivals if only because of their respective fishing interests.

However, the match was destined not to take place at Fleetwood. The club was in financial trouble and the Hull club offered to pay £40, plus a share of the gate, to switch the tie. It was a decision which did not please many local people, who were always looking to put one over on the rival port, but did make sound financial sense. After a six hour train journey it was a match Fleetwood really could not hope to win and was lost 0-31. Beaten the players may have been, but they had not been disgraced, a point taken up by the local reporter who travelled with them to the game. "Fleetwood dropped heavily at Hull but what could be expected of a one year infant against a team of internationals....it was the quick short passing of the forwards which completely nonplussed the Fleetwood men as well as the strong rushes....one of the Fleetwood men likened these rushes to a cavalry charge and said it was almost as impossible to stop them....fancy facing forwards none less than 5'11" and about 13 stones each! No wonder they carried all before them."

On 13 November 1897 the Fleetwood players, along with 150 supporters, boarded the steamer Lune to sail across Morecambe Bay to play a match against Barrow. The "Barrow boat" sailed quite frequently to and fro between the two ports so it must have seemed a good idea to the committee. Sadly no one checked with the players as the reporter said "Rugby players they may be but sailors they most certainly are not." The crossing must have been quite rough for most of the players were seasick and Barrow had an easy 30-0 victory.

The committee obviously did not learn from its mistake as the players repeated the journey on 22 January 1898, when they sailed to Barrow, boarded wagonettes to the station and then continued by train to Ulverston. The result was similar, as Fleetwood lost 5-36.

The second season opened with a 19-3 win at newcomers Blackpool but, generally, the trend remained the same. Fleetwood won the return match and also gained a point from a home game against Ulverston but only Blackpool's failings prevented another wooden spoon. Victories, both home and away, against Walkden were later expunged from the table when the *Stocksmen* disbanded.

In the Challenge Cup Fleetwood played Blackpool, in the preliminary round, the first and only time that two Fylde Coast clubs were to meet in the competition. Fleetwood proved too strong winning 13-8 to earn a trip to Widnes in the first round, when Fleetwood went down heavily 3-48. As the season drew to a close Fleetwood's future appeared less than rosy but had at least survived longer than the Blackpool club which had disbanded.

Fleetwood was finding it increasingly difficult to make any real headway, as the supply of players from senior clubs began to dry up. The senior clubs could afford to pay wages even to their reserve team players, so it was not financially worthwhile for such players to leave and join the smaller clubs.

The end of the century sounded the death-knell of the Fleetwood club and yet, ironically, the 1899-1900 season which was the last full campaign, was the most successful in playing terms. The club did manage to enter the transfer market buying a first-class Welsh wingman, E Spillane, from Leigh and Ulverston's star full-back, Fred Moran. Spillane made an immediate impression notching both tries as Fleetwood began the season with a 6-6 draw at home to Werneth. The following Saturday saw Fleetwood travel to Barrow, again by boat. Another rough crossing was endured and Fleetwood lost 0-24.

At last Fleetwood proved to be a competitive force and won six and drew three of its 19 league games. A home 3-3 draw against eventual champions Barrow was the best performance. In other games Fleetwood often lost by the narrowest of margins preventing it rising above an eventual eighth place.

A "Barrow boat" similar to the "Lune" which was in service in 1897. (Photograph courtesy Mrs Bill Curtis)

Supporters on the "Barrow boat" at Fleetwood as it prepares to set sail across Morecambe Bay.(Photograph courtesy Mrs Bill Curtis)

The club had scouted for players as far afield as South Wales, signing a full-back, Jenkins, who was reputed to be a reserve for the international team and a winger, Freeman. Both players soon attracted the attention of a number of senior clubs and Fleetwood was unable to keep the pair. Jenkins was transferred to Oldham before the year was out and he was quickly followed by Freeman who was reluctantly allowed to sign for Hull.

The season ended with a notable double success over Lancaster which proved that Fleetwood was, at last, beginning to compete with the big boys. Sadly it proved too late for the club as other forces, over which it had no control, were beginning to take effect. As the season drew to its close the death-knell was beginning to sound even louder.

As the 1900-01 season began the club was on its last legs. The Copse Ground had been sold to developers and the association club had moved further into the centre of the town. For some reason the rugby club could not, or would not, go with it but returned to the original base in Thornton. Support, which was already dwindling, reduced further after the move. Travelling expenses were high and professionalism had removed many players out of the reach of the pocket of the club. The club played its last two matches at the Copse Ground before the developers moved in, losing 0-6 to Werneth and 0-7 to Leigh St Joseph's in the first round of the Lancashire Junior Cup.

The club's last home game, played at Cardwell's Field, Thornton on 22 December 1900 ended in a defeat, 0-13, at the hands of Lancaster. In the first three months of the season Fleetwood had fulfilled only five league fixtures losing four and drawing 0-0 at home to Whitworth.

The *Leigh Journal* reported on 19 January 1901 that "the Fleetwood club is now defunct. It has struggled on for a number of years and this season has been beset by difficulties. The players were unwilling to play unless they were better paid than the club's resources allowed while the public have not supported to any extent by attending matches."

With Fleetwood's passing, professional rugby left the Fylde Coast and did not return for over 50 years when Blackpool Borough came into existence.

Lancaster

FOUNDED: c. 1877
CEASED: 1905
REASON: financial problems and difficulties in arranging fixtures
GROUND: Quay Meadow
HEADQUARTERS: Queen's Hotel
COLOURS: Red and white

THE Lancaster club was founded when a number of sportsmen in the town began to play as a scratch team. First evidence of a definite date comes from local newspaper sources. The *Lancaster Guardian*, writing on the winding up of the club, stated: "For a long period, something like thirty-five years in fact, rugby football has been the paramount interest of the district....The old Lancaster Club played on the Giant Axe Field...."

This puts the club's formation around 1870 but at this time rugby, if it were played, would have been on an ad hoc basis. Perhaps a more accurate assessment can be gleaned from a report on the Lancaster club's annual dinner in the *Lancashire Daily Post* in 1897. The Mayor of Lancaster said that it was twenty years since the club was formed and prior to that he had played in a number of scratch sides. This places the start of the club around 1877.

What does become apparent is that Lancaster soon gained considerable local support and became the premier club in the district though, by the early 1890's, Morecambe had become a great rival. In 1892-93 Lancaster enjoyed a marvellous season and with 12 wins, 3 draws and only one defeat won the North-Western League one point ahead of runners-up Millom and three points clear of Morecambe. Lancaster now played at Quay Meadow. The ground was very picturesque, overlooked by the castle and St Mary's church. On visiting the site, which remains open land, it is easy to envisage the days when rugby was played there.

Lancaster regularly undertook tours of South Wales and on one visit, in October 1896, played Llanelli. Gareth Hughes, in his book, "*The Scarlets*" wrote: "When Lancaster played at Stradey in October one of their forwards John Pinch, an English International, was sent off. He was warned twice for using abusive language to the referee. He did it a third time and was sent off." Pinch was to be Lancaster's first and only Rugby Union international and was also influential in the club's decision to join the Northern Union in 1897.

In the 1892-93 season when league rugby, to a certain extent, was forced upon the Lancashire County Rugby Union committee following the formation of the Yorkshire Senior Competition, Lancaster found itself at the forefront of the junior clubs which were pushing to be included in such a league. The following season the club became a founder member of the Lancashire Club Championship (Second Class) finishing in mid-table.

As a result of the turmoil in the summer of 1895, the Lancaster club found itself thrust into the spotlight of the Lancashire First Class ranks, something that must have been viewed with mixed emotions. For John Pinch the breakaway, which rendered the Northern Union players ineligible for Rugby Union internationals, allowed him to taste tremendous success. In 1896 he was selected to play for England. In total he was to win three caps, the last in 1897, the same year the club joined the Northern Union. EB Thompson and C Danby also represented Lancashire while F Hoggarth and W Hall played for Westmorland.

The 1896-97 season was to be the last for the Lancaster club in the Rugby Union. With some reluctance the club decided that, finan-

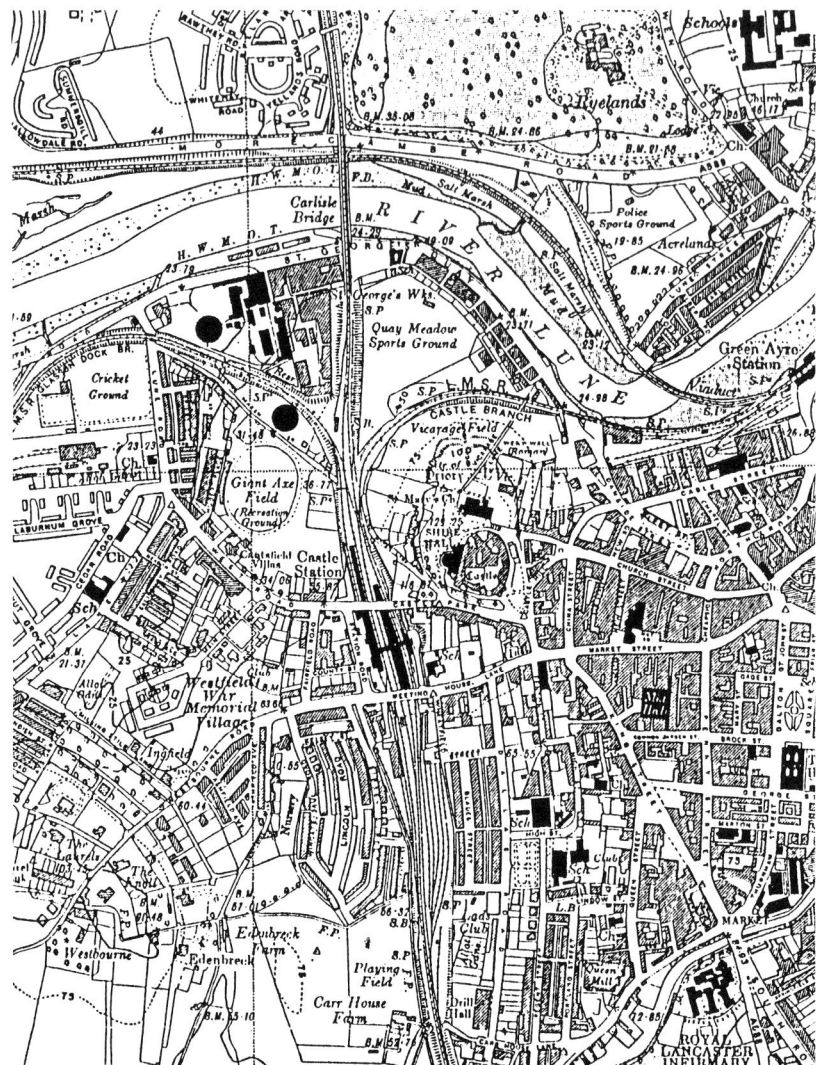

Quay Meadow and Lancaster's original pitch at Giant Axe. Both fields are still in use today, the former as a playing field, the latter as the home of Lancaster AFC. Earlier maps show the Quay Meadow but do not name it as such. (Reproduced from 1936 Ordnance Survey Map)

cially, it could no longer survive within the Rugby Union and decided to seek membership of the Lancashire Second Competition of the Northern Union.

On the first day of the 1897-98 season the fixtures determined that one of Lancashire's oldest clubs played one of its youngest, Fleetwood. The match was played at Quay Meadow in front of a crowd of around 2000 and Lancaster won 14-5. This first season saw Lancaster make a solid, rather than spectacular, beginning in the Northern Union. This was to prove typical of the club's fortunes throughout its time in the Second Competition and Lancaster was destined to spend most of the time in mid-table. In the last season spent in the Second Competition, Lancaster went through unbeaten at Quay Meadow but could not manage to win a single game away from home.

What was happening, quite simply, was that Lancaster was not having the success that the supporters wanted and had been used to, prior to the Northern Union days, albeit that the playing standard was now much higher. Lancaster's finances were a cause for concern and some good fortune came when Lord Ashton, "to show his appreciation of the management of the club steering clear of the close affinity with public houses that marks some clubs" decided to wipe off debts of over £100.

By the end of the 1900-01 season Lancaster, along with everyone else, was glad to see the back of the Lancashire Second Competition. Travelling expenses were proving to be astronomical in comparison with the gate receipts. After one season of competing in the Lancashire Senior Competition, filling one of the places left vacant by the clubs which formed their own, short-lived Northern League, Lancaster became a founder member of the inter-county Second Division.

Lancaster was again playing many senior clubs it had last met on a regular basis in the Rugby Union days but the passing years had not been kind to Lancaster or, more precisely, had been much kinder to many of its rivals.

Lancaster forward John Pinch, who won three caps for the England Rugby Union side. (Photograph courtesy Tim Auty)

Lancaster went through the 1901-02 season winning only eight league games. What was apparent from that season was that Lancaster had one jewel shining brightly in a struggling team and this was Jimmy Leytham, who was destined to become one of the finest players of his or any other era. Leytham was destined for great things not with Lancaster but with Wigan.

The first campaign of the Second Division in 1902-03 saw Lancaster start with wins against Dewsbury, South Shields, Bramley, Castleford and Normanton, drawing with Rochdale Hornets. Lancaster was undefeated going into the third Saturday in October when its colours were lowered by Manningham. Though fortunes declined, the season saw the side finish in eleventh position with 13 wins, 4 draws and 17 defeats. Lancaster had held its own but a growing and worrying trend of falling gates was apparent, particularly to the new association game, which was growing in strength in the Lancaster district.

The travelling expenses were so high that gate money was needed more than ever but the problem was that many of the Yorkshire clubs which competed in the league were not considered great attractions. For that matter nor was Lancaster when it ventured across the Pennines. The lack of games against Lancashire teams was a major source of the financial difficulties now faced by the Lancaster committee.

The 1903-04 season saw a decline in the club's fortunes as only eight wins and two draws were gained in 32 league games and the outstanding Leytham was transferred in December 1903. In the Challenge Cup Lancaster had managed to beat Morecambe in the intermediate round but needed a replay to do so. Lancaster progressed no further losing 0-8 at home to Keighley in the first round. The following season saw a similar sort of story and, yet again, a quick exit in the cup 7-24 at Castleford. Lancaster saved some of its best form for the last month of the campaign and ended with a 5-0 home win over Rochdale Hornets on 22 April 1905, the fourth success in six games. However, once again, events beyond control were beginning to have a say in matters.

The system of two divisions was a financial disaster for many clubs, not only for Lancaster, and it was decided to revert back to a single division in the Senior Competition for the 1905-06 season. There were far too many clubs to allow each to play the other home and away, and the Northern Union committee faced a dilemma which, on the face of it, it did not know how to tackle. The answer was simply to adopt a policy which suited the committee and left the junior clubs with nowhere to go.

The authorities gave club secretaries the freedom to arrange their own fixtures with the stipulation that a minimum of twenty league games was fulfilled. It was also a requirement that clubs could not refuse fixtures against a club from its own county which had been in the same division the previous season. Lancaster's problem was that there had not been ten Lancashire teams in the Second Division but only four in Millom, Barrow, Rochdale Hornets and Morecambe. Lancaster's geographical location and low profile did not make it an attractive date on the fixture card.

The smaller clubs such as Lancaster suffered badly as a result of this policy decision and the result was a crisis from which many could not hope to recover. The plight of Lancaster was well documented and makes unpleasant reading.

The *Lancaster Guardian* first carried news of the problems facing the club in their edition of 10 June 1905 under the headline:

"NORTHERN UNION FOOTBALL CRISIS."

The club had mounting debts and was struggling to make ends meet. The travelling expenses in their previous season had come to £77 and broken-time payments £33. Things were in such a bad state that, at the AGM, there were no nominations for the committee so really nothing could be formulated for the coming season. That, however, was not the only problem as the report went on to show:

"Mr W Huntington: Have you any idea what the new scheme for the Northern League is going to be? Will there be a second division? The Chairman said as far as he could understand there would be neither a first nor second division. The principle of the scheme was the same as adopted in first-class cricket. A club could arrange fixtures with whom they liked but they had to play so many first-class fixtures or drop out of the league. It meant that Lancaster would have to arrange fixtures with at least ten clubs and where they would find them he did not know.

"There was Millom, Barrow and Morecambe but beyond that he did not know who they would get to come to Lancaster. Wigan would not come, St Helens were very much in the same box and the Yorkshire clubs, Normanton, Bramley and so on would be able to arrange with clubs in their own county. Clubs would refuse to come to Lancaster on account of the heavy travelling expenses. The travelling expenses of the Lancaster club were equal to those of most first division clubs. In reply to further questions the chairman said the second division clubs had never been consulted, it was purely a first division scheme and they had never been able to get a satisfactory decision amongst themselves....some of the Yorkshire clubs said they would disband rather than take Lancaster on their card. There were not sufficient clubs in North Lancashire to enable Lancaster to get fixtures.

"Mr G Jackson: I thought the scheme was adopted for the benefit of the second division clubs. It seems to me they are going to be wiped out."

No decision was taken at that meeting as to the course of action to take but a further meeting was to be held a week later. It was at this meeting that the Lancaster club was to end its days. Once again there was no-one prepared to stand for the committee and take responsibility for a club with debts which now stood at around £100, with no prospect of getting enough matches to stay in the Northern Union. Consequently, the club was allowed to go under and this as a result of the actions or, more accurately, the inaction of the governing body of the Northern Union.

As Mr Burtholme, a committee man and former player of great standing, stated so poignantly at the end of the newspaper article: "They have killed the game in the district." The Lancaster club went out of existence on 17 June 1905 and the professional game never returned to the Lancaster area.

Leigh Shamrocks

FOUNDED: 1889
CEASED: 1914
REASON: Lack of players due to start of World War One
GROUND: Buck's Farm
HEADQUARTERS: Bridge Inn
COLOURS: Green jersey with white collar and cuffs, blue shorts

Leigh Shamrocks soon became known as a good junior club in the Lancashire area. The home ground was at Buck's Farm where the fledgling Leigh club had played in its early days in the late 1870's. The Shamrocks side, as the name implies, comprised largely, though not exclusively, Leigh Irishmen, there being a large Irish community in the town around that time.

Headquarters was at the Bridge Inn, a few hundred yards from the ground, and the club acquired various nicknames, the Rocks, Irishmen and the Bridge Lads among them.

Shamrocks came to the forefront of junior circles when it won the South East Lancashire and Border Towns Junior Cup in March 1893 defeating Pendleton Hornets at Bradford and Clayton FC ground, Manchester, in front of a crowd of 2000.

The following season Shamrocks looked to be well on the way towards retaining the cup after wins over Castleton Moor, Standish South End and Manchester Athletic until the club committee decided to withdraw from the competition following a dispute.

Shamrocks finished as runners-up in the South West Lancashire League in 1894-95 and in the following season the club was elected to join the Second Class of the Lancashire Club Championship, due to the large number of vacancies left by those which departed to form the breakaway Northern Union. Shamrocks performed with great credit being in contention for the championship until the last few games. Shamrocks finished in joint second place, alongside Radcliffe and Barton, two points behind eventual winners Mossley.

In 1896-97 Shamrocks found itself promoted to the First Class due, in no small part, to the shortage of clubs now competing under the Rugby Union banner in Lancashire. The other clubs in the league were Littleborough, Barton, Blackley Rangers, Mossley, Castleton Moor, Whitworth, Cheetham Hill, Rochdale Rangers and Boothstown. Shamrocks forward T Tickle became the first, and only, player from the club to win Lancashire county honours during the season.

Shamrocks was again justifying the elevation when, in the *Leigh Journal* of 19 March 1897, it was announced that "the Leigh Shamrocks committee have unanimously decided to follow the lead of Barton and Blackley Rangers and join the Northern Union. The decision is something of a surprise as Shamrocks are runners-up in the league at this juncture and in with a good chance of reaching the semi-final of the cup, but next season a Lancashire Second and possibly Third Competition is to be formed." Shamrocks was offered a place in the Second Competition but chose to compete in the Third in an attempt to reduce travelling expenses.

In 1897-98 Shamrocks endured the worst-ever season both financially and in a playing sense. Local rival Boothstown folded after playing a few league games but Shamrocks, by keeping a tight rein on expenses, was able to carry on. "It is to the credit of the Buck's Farm organisation that they exist on such slender resources" commented the *Leigh Journal*.

Shamrocks opted not to pay broken-time expenses and getting a side together for

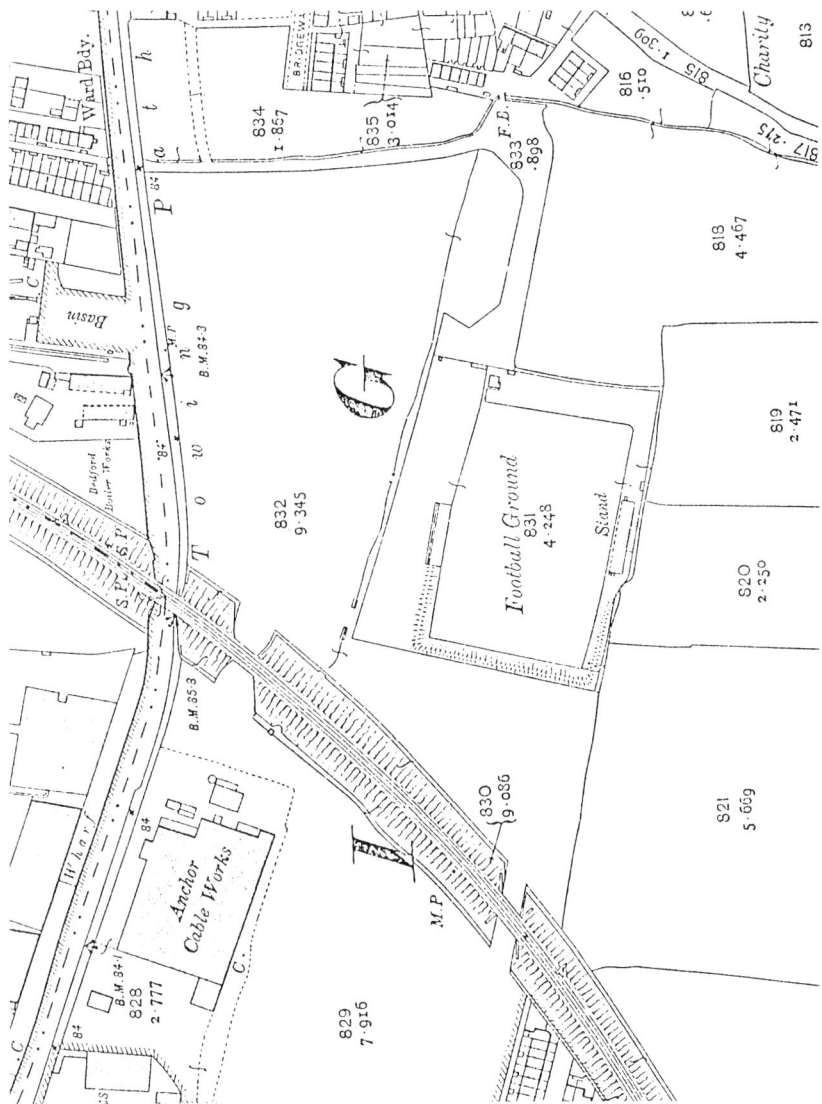

Leigh Shamrocks played on a field marked by map reference 829. On the other side of the railway line was Leigh's Mather Lane ground. (Reproduced from 1893 Ordnance Survey Map)

away games was a recurrent problem. Several of the side who worked in the collieries were simply unable to leave work in time for away games and for home fixtures turned up straight from the shift still covered in pit dirt.

Long before the season was out Shamrocks decided to join the Manchester League in 1898-99. After being a clear leader in the new competition, the club again had a joust with authority withdrawing in protest "at the erratic ruling of the league committee."

In 1899-1900 Shamrocks competed in the Lancashire Junior Division before being invited to join the Lancashire Second Competition in 1900-01. This was a major step-up for the club as it would now come into contact with a number of larger organisations, including the fallen local giant Tyldesley. Shamrocks always appeared to enjoy a good working relationship with the town's senior club and the committee got together with its counterpart at Mather Lane to ensure that Shamrocks' and Leigh's home league fixtures did not clash.

Sadly Shamrocks was out of its depth in many games even though it was never defeated by disastrous margins. The opening fixture proved to be a rude awakening when faced by a powerful Birkenhead Wanderers side and lost 0-18. Only one other defeat, 2-22 at Altrincham, was by a greater score. "Hardly a bed of roses" was how the Leigh Journal summarised the campaign.

Home wins were earned against Altrincham and Lancaster as Shamrocks, when able to field its strongest side, was capable of competing satisfactorily. Even then playing methods did not gain approval. "The Shamrocks do not play a scientific game which true lovers of the game like to see" stated the Leigh Journal.

Absences were the big problem for, as well as the problem of players being unable to leave work, four of the club's most prominent players, Murray, Coyne, Collins and Lynch were lost to the forces serving in the South African War. It was not uncommon for Shamrocks to start away games with eleven or twelve men with the numbers being made up when more players arrived by a later train.

Attendances were disappointing, numbering only a few hundred for most games. The lack of cover on the Buck's Farm enclosure meant that watching games in bad weather was a far from happy experience. The long-awaited Christmas home clash against Tyldesley coincided with a day of steady rain and howling winds keeping the attendance down to 200.

With Fleetwood disbanding during the season, Shamrocks played only 16 league games and had finished its programme by mid-January, hardly a satisfactory situation. "There is little point in carrying on in the Second Competition" commented the Leigh Journal, though Shamrocks' loss for the season, £1, was a modest one. Gate receipts for the campaign had totalled only £70.

Shamrocks finished bottom of the table with only four league points scoring 33 points and conceding 157. In 16 games Shamrocks scored only five tries. Full-back Caveney, half-backs MacMasters and Rabbitt, three-quarter Shovelton and forwards Roberts and Riley were Shamrocks' most prominent players but over 40 players turned out during the season as the club was rarely able to field a settled side.

In the summer of 1901, Shamrocks was accepted into the newly-formed Central Lancashire League, alongside Leigh St Joseph's, Westleigh Catholics, Tyldesley Shamrocks, Westleigh, Pendlebury, Flixton, Glenby Hornets, Castleton Moor, Salford St Bart's, Rochdale Rangers, Abbey Hills and Lees. The club resumed its place among the junior ranks providing a useful nursery for the town's senior team and other professional outfits. Chief amongst the many Shamrocks players to turn professional was a classy half-back, Bert Ganley, who played with distinction for Leigh, Huddersfield and Leeds.

In 1904-05 Shamrocks won its way through the qualifying rounds to reach the first round of the Challenge Cup losing 0-52 to Hull. The following season Shamrocks again appeared in the first round losing to fellow junior club Egerton at Salford.

In 1907-08 Shamrocks again moved up in status when the club was rewarded for its consistently good record in the junior game by being invited to join the Lancashire Rugby Combination. It joined other local amateur clubs Wigan Highfield, Ince and Pemberton and competed against the reserve teams of the county's senior clubs.

Games against Leigh A and Wigan A attracted good crowds to Buck's Farm and Shamrocks competed most effectively attaining fourth place in 1908-09 with 11 wins and 5 draws from 24 games. The league was later amalgamated with its counterpart in Yorkshire to form a Northern Rugby Combination with positions being decided on a percentage basis. Wigan Highfield, Pemberton, Normanton St Jude's, Purston and Millom were the other junior clubs involved.

Leigh Shamrocks had established for itself a fine reputation and the club was the leading amateur organisation in a town which was, and indeed still is, a stronghold of the game. The start of the First World War in 1914 signalled the club's demise. Most of the players either joined the forces or were serving in reserved occupations and the club, suddenly without any playing members, was wound up.

Millom

FOUNDED: 1873
CEASED: 1906
REASON: reverted to amateur ranks
GROUND: Salthouse
HEADQUARTERS: Millom Castle Hotel
COLOURS: Navy blue

MILLOM was one of the oldest and most successful clubs in Cumberland at the time of the decision to switch over to the Northern Union. It joined the Cumberland County Union in 1885 and won the Cumberland Challenge Cup in three successive seasons in the late 1880's. When the North-Western League was formed in the season 1891-92 Millom earned the title of inaugural champions. The players were champions again in 1893-94 and 1896-97 and runners-up in 1892-93, 1894-95 and 1895-96.

The decision was not one taken in isolation for, with neighbouring clubs such as Barrow and Ulverston either having decided to join, or being on the verge of joining the Northern Union, Millom could have been left high and dry. Following a general meeting of members at the Central Hall in July 1897 it was unanimously decided to switch codes. Millom was immediately allocated a place in the Lancashire Second Competition and regarded as championship favourites along with Barrow.

Ironically, at the time, Millom had reached a high standing in Rugby Union circles, confirmed when forward Edward Knowles was chosen to represent England against Scotland in March 1896.

In the 1896-97 season, Cumberland reached the final of the County Championship losing 3-9 to Kent at Carlisle in April 1897. The county side included no less than eight Millom players, full-back J Buckett, three-quarters J Young, R Moore and W Cunningham, half-backs S Northmore and T James and forwards Knowles and S Hoggarth. Seaton, Carlisle, Aspatria and Workington were the other clubs to provide players for the county.

Northmore, Knowles and Hoggarth all represented the North of England against the South at Dewsbury and Northmore and Knowles were chosen for England. Northmore played against Ireland at Dublin while Knowles earned his second cap against Scotland at Manchester.

Millom also won the North-Western Cup for the third time yet, despite all successes, lost £50 in gate money during the season.

Millom's first game under Northern Union rules was the opening league fixture against Barton at Salthouse on 4 September 1897. The visitors held a 9-0 lead at half-time before

Millom half-back Sam Nothmore prior to representing England against Ireland in 1897. (Photograph courtesy Tim Auty)

Millom

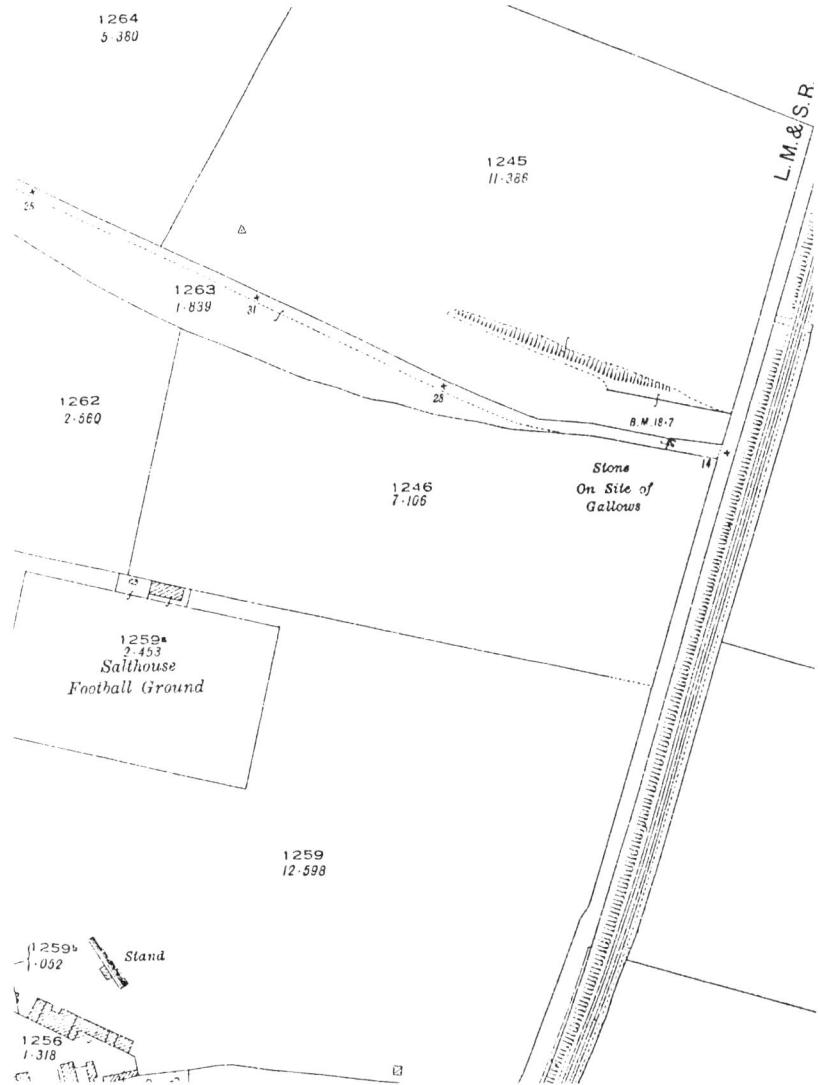

The Salthouse Ground. An earlier map shows the grandstand but nothing else, suggesting that in 1892 the ground was still being laid out. From the map it appears that access was somewhat difficult, as no road is shown. (Reproduced from 1897 Ordnance Survey Map)

Millom recovered to win 15-9 with tries by Northmore, Young and Smetheram.

The new league forced Millom to face a number of long train journeys necessitating an early morning start. While many of the Lancashire and Cheshire clubs complained at the travelling costs incurred in getting to the Cumbrian coastal town, Millom had to make long journeys every other week.

Unlike some of the other clubs in the league Millom relied on local talent, keeping together the side which had served them well in the Rugby Union days. Millom's players formed the bulk of the Cumberland Northern Union side with no less than twelve appearing in the county side which lost 0-8 to Yorkshire at Hunslet in February 1898.

Not only a capable side, but one which played enterprisingly, Millom justified its pre-season billing yet suffered some surprise defeats, losing both home and away against Altrincham and St Helens Recs, and began to lag behind Barrow in the table. It was Recs' decision to disband late in the season which opened up the league. Recs' results were expunged and Barrow, which had beaten Recs once, saw Millom emerge as strong challengers.

Millom drew level with their great rivals on 27 points when they beat them 7-0 in the final league game on 16 April 1898. Before a ground record crowd of 4000, realising receipts of £111, a try by Knowles and goals by Young and Buckett decided the issue.

The two clubs were ordered to play-off for the championship at Askam on Thursday 28 April with the winners to play Morecambe in the test match at Lancaster two days later. The game at Askam was an intense struggle, played before 4000 spectators, and in fading light ended scoreless. The play-off went to a second game at Lancaster the following Saturday, the test being put back one week and past the normal end of season mark of 30 April. This time Barrow was victorious 2-0.

Despite the disappointment, Millom felt its decision to join the Northern Union had been fully vindicated. It was reported that only five of the senior clubs in Cumberland, Whitehaven, Aspatria, Penrith, Cockermouth and Carlisle had remained loyal to the Rugby Union. Gate receipts totalled £284 and a profit of £61 was made despite railway fares of £130 and broken-time payments of £97.

In the 1898-99 season Millom swept all before it, holding off another strong challenge from Barrow, whose attempt at first-class status had met with disappointment. Millom dropped only one league point, in a scoreless draw at Altrincham, and not only piled up some high scores but maintained a mean defence. In no less than 13 of their 16 league games, Millom kept its opponents' scoresheets blank.

League newcomer Blackpool was given a particularly rude awakening conceding 119 points without reply in the two games. Millom winger Young scored five of his side's 14 tries in their 52-0 win at Raikes Hall then went one better with six out of 17 tries in the 67-0 thrashing at Salthouse.

Millom played Morecambe, which again finished bottom of the Lancashire Senior Competition, in a test match at Salford's New Barns ground. Neither the venue nor date, a Wednesday afternoon 26 April, were ideal for players or supporters of the two clubs but doubtless the arrangements were more than satisfactory for the majority of the committee members of the Lancashire Northern Union who organised the game.

Millom earned the right to play in the senior league with an emphatic 11-3 victory. Northmore scored the only try of the first-half and after the interval Young and Smetheram went over, Buckett kicking a goal. Morecambe's only response was a late try by Hadwen. The Millom side was: Eagers; Young, Whitehead, Leck, Latham; Northmore, Wharton; Knowles, Buckett, Hoggarth, Fawcett, Kitchen, Smetheram, Grenfell, Scott.

Millom's success had been complemented with a perfect record in the North-Western League with 14 wins over Barrow, Workington, Dalton, Maryport, Ulverston, Lancaster and Askam.

The new season was looked upon with

great enthusiasm as Millom attempted to consolidate in the Senior Competition. There was great pride in the town that success had been achieved without the assistance of outsiders. Millom achieved its aim, finishing 12th out of 14 clubs with seven wins and a draw in 26 league games.

The Blues enjoyed their best season in the Northern Union in 1902-03. In this season the county leagues were abandoned and two divisions introduced. Millom, competing in the second division, finished third out of 18 clubs with 22 wins and three draws in 34 league games. Winger T Gartrell, with 21 tries, was third in the overall scoring lists.

A sign of the financial burden of competing in a league which now involved a number of trips into Yorkshire, all to be paid for out of home gates which were often numbered in their hundreds, came when Millom gave up home advantage after reaching the third round of the Challenge Cup. Millom accepted Hull's offer of a financial guarantee and effectively said farewell to hopes of further progress, losing 0-7.

In the following two seasons, Millom competed with a reasonable amount of success finishing 12th and 7th in the second division. The system of two divisions was ended in 1905 and the decision to revert to a single league was to signal a decisive blow for smaller, isolated clubs, such as Millom.

The new 31-strong Northern League, which was to be decided on a percentage basis, had the pre-condition that clubs had to complete home and away fixtures against ten member clubs. Secretaries were left to organise their own fixtures and, under the new scheme, Millom had enormous difficulties in persuading the requisite number of clubs to make the long and costly journey to the north-west coast in return for a home fixture against a club regarded as unfashionable and hence unlikely to attract a big gate.

Significantly Millom played only the minimum 20 league games. Only Oldham, Leigh, Wigan, St Helens, Warrington, Rochdale Hornets and Runcorn were persuaded to play Millom from the Lancashire and Cheshire heartland while Millom's only fixtures against a Yorkshire club were arranged against Pontefract. Aside from local games against Barrow and Morecambe, Millom's secretary was left scratching around.

Inevitably fixtures were irregular with Millom enduring a gap of seven weeks in the autumn without a league game and only three wins, over Morecambe, Rochdale Hornets and Pontefract and two draws were earned. Even so Millom finished in 27th place with daylight between itself and the bottom spot.

Millom's final game as a senior club was on Saturday 28 April 1906 when Pontefract was defeated 10-5 at Salthouse. Millom won 75, drew 10 and lost 103 of its 188 league games as a senior club, a respectable record, but problems with fixtures, the long distance travel and broken-time payments all combined to bring Millom's days as a senior club to an end.

From 1906-07 *the Blues* reverted to the amateur ranks competing in the Cumberland Senior League. Millom continued to provide players for the county side and Salthouse was the venue for a county game against Yorkshire in December 1911. A crowd of 3500 saw Cumberland, including Millom players J Morgan and T Price, win 16-13.

Millom also reached the first round of the Challenge Cup on a further four occasions before the First World War.

In the space of ten years or so Millom had begun to slide from a side at the top of the game, with two England internationals in its ranks, to a club forced by circumstances to abandon senior status after a perennial struggle for survival. "Clubs growl at the journey to Millom" stated the *Altrincham Guardian* in 1900 and it was this factor, the unwillingness of many of the senior clubs to accommodate Millom's geographical isolation, which was the biggest single contributor to its demise.

Fortunately the game was not lost to the town and Millom continues to be a stronghold of rugby league.

Morecambe

FOUNDED: 1876
CEASED: 1906
REASON: financial problems and difficulties in arranging fixtures
GROUND: Moss Lane
HEADQUARTERS: King's Arms Hotel
COLOURS: Royal blue and white striped jerseys, white shorts

THE Morecambe club was formed a few years before its local rival inland being Lancaster. The game began to make great strides forward in the early 1880's and Morecambe was no exception. The club quickly became settled at the King's Arms Hotel in the town and acquired the use of a piece of land owned by the railway company at Moss Lane. The club had a permanent home ground and spectators in the town supported the club in encouraging numbers.

Morecambe was one of the few clubs which seemed to stay loyal to its original state and once settled did not move from ground to ground or, for that matter, change colours. By the late 1880's it had built up an attractive fixture list and became one of the most successful clubs in the north of the county.

When a Rugby Union Lancashire Club Championship arrived in 1892 Morecambe found itself in a state of limbo and it was not until the 1894-95 season that it was invited to join the Third Class Competition. *The Seasiders*, as the club was known, had competed in the North-Western League from its inception but now had the opportunity to increase its standing on a less parochial level.

Morecambe acquitted itself well, finishing a creditable third behind Pemberton and Crompton, despite failing to fulfil three of its fixtures. Morecambe was happy enough as it must have felt it was making up lost ground on Lancaster who, much to its dismay, were in the Second Class Competition.

Morecambe suddenly found itself elevated to the dizzy heights of the First Class Competition for the following season, due to the gaps left by the breakaway Northern Union clubs. Much to the surprise of a great many people Morecambe enjoyed perhaps the best season in its history and won the league, by five clear points, from runners-up Ulverston with third-placed Lancaster trailing in twelve points behind.

The club's record was a formidable one with 18 wins, a draw and only one defeat in 20 games. Morecambe also ran away with the North-Western League title dropping only one point in twelve fixtures. Both cups were presented to the club captain Adam Elkin before a game against Millom late in the season. Full-back Elkin and half-back Tommy Dent both gave nearly twenty years service to the club and with "Bratty" Holmes, James Altham, Herbert Hadwen and Bobby Lewis were the stalwarts.

Buoyed by this unexpected success Morecambe applied for a place in the Lancashire Senior Competition of the Northern Union. To Morecambe's surprise it was granted a place and thus, in the space of a couple of years, had enjoyed a rapid rise in status. The Morecambe committee, by switching to the Northern Union, thought it had accurately gauged the way the land lay for clubs in the north of the county and changed while the going was good.

The *Lancaster Guardian* of 26 August 1896 rather disdainfully reported the Morecambe defection and published its fixture list along with the following comment. "It is old news now that Morecambe have been elected to the first division of the Lancashire section of the Northern Union and their list of engage-

Morecambe

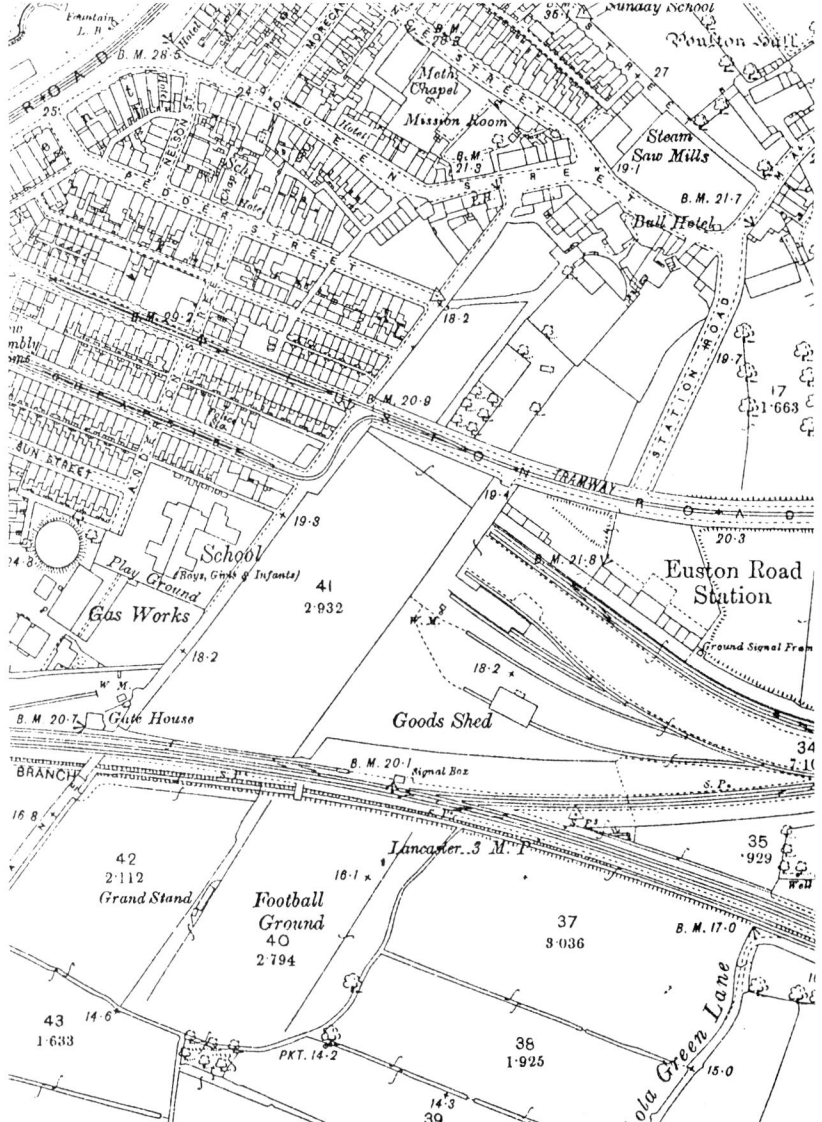

The Morecambe ground at Moss Lane. The ground was rented from the Railway Company, whose line ran alongside it. The fact that the Railway wanted the land back in 1906 resulted in the ultimate demise of the club. (Reproduced from 1894 Ordnance Survey Map)

ments comprises fixtures with all the leading Northern Union clubs. The first team players are, I understand, practising nightly and the committee has every prospect of placing in the field a very strong fifteen...."

In the first season in the Northern Union, Morecambe struggled in elevated company and won only three league games. In the cup, having been drawn at home to Bramley, the club gave up ground advantage for a gate guarantee and gained a creditable 8-8 draw. The replay, also played at Bramley, resulted in a 4-6 defeat. The team was basically the same as that of the previous season and, as a result, did as well as could be expected.

At the AGM it was revealed that Morecambe had broken even on the season. In the last few years of its membership of the Rugby Union, debts had been steadily growing and at last some progress in reversing the financial decline could be seen. Morecambe could now look forward to the coming season with some confidence that it would survive financially.

With largely the same team as the previous term Morecambe again had little or no success and, once more, finished bottom of the Lancashire Senior Competition. Morecambe did, however, manage four wins during the campaign and a further two draws, one of them 5-5 at St Helens. The match was recorded in the *Morecambe Visitor* on 20 April 1898 and, from all accounts rugby matches, at least for Morecambe, appear to have been good days out for all concerned:-

"The fifteen players accompanied by Mr JC Turner and "Nemo" (the reporter) left Morecambe by the 10.15 train and arrived in St Helens just after 12 o'clock. Dinner was the first thing thought of and by the time this little matter had received proper attention it was turned 1 o'clock. So there remained an hour or so to be killed before making tracks for the hostelry, presided over by Billy Cross, the headquarters of the Saints. A considerable amount of time was spent in the glass market where numerous purchases were made.... subsequently we stumbled across a weigh-

Morecambe photographed with the Lancashire Club Championship and North-Western League cups in 1896.
Back row: A Duff, W Cornthwaite, R Holmes, R Batty, A Elkin, P Wilson, G Hadwen, J Altham, T Campbell, J Holmes. **Middle row:** J Hayton, S Thornton, J Benson, H Hadwen, H Gardner, R Lewis. **Front row:** W Blacow, T Dent.
(Photograph courtesy Tim Auty)

ing machine and, at a penny a time, players had their "Krect" weight recorded...."

The combined weight of the fifteen-strong team, incidentally, was 173 stones 4 pounds or an average weight of eleven and a half stones. Compared to the teams of today they would appear to be quite small.

Nemo continued "The St Helens ground is about three miles from the centre of the town and the men after donning the habiliments of war had a pleasant ride to the scene of the encounter. One of the touch-judges failed to put in an appearance and the captains tossed up as to who should wave the flag on high.....the Morecambrian committee man figured as the touch line artist....

"In consequence of the club colours of the Saints being practically identical to those of the *Seasiders*, the home team were obliged to make a change and a rare mixture they appeared in, red and green, amber and black and all white, three distinct sets....The first moiety of thirty five minutes was opened by Cornthwaite........"

The report of the match continues in the same leisurely fashion, certainly a much pleasanter approach to the game seems to have been adopted than is the case today.

The consequence of finishing bottom of the league was that the club had to play a test match against Barrow, the champions of the Lancashire Second Competition. This was staged on 7 May at Quay Meadow, Lancaster. Morecambe won a hard, tense encounter 10-0 preserving senior status. Barrow had been involved in two bruising encounters with Millom for the right to meet Morecambe in the test match and a third game in ten days proved too much for the team.

Whilst struggling on the field, off it the club was having more success. A report in the *Barrow News* of 18 June 1898, of Morecambe's AGM showed that the club was back in the black: "The balance sheet of the Morecambe club, which will be issued in the course of a few days, is one which the "wooden spoonists"....may well be pleased.....despite the unenviable position they held at the close, there has been a gain of £51 on the year's working, an adverse balance at the beginning of the season of £43 being converted into a credit balance of £8...."

From the brief report it is possible to get some idea of the workings of a club struggling in the bottom reaches of the Senior Competition. Gate receipts for the season amounted to £257. In the cup Morecambe played Hull away and half the share of the gate realised £82. On the debit side, the club paid out for such items as referee's fees and touch judges £37, while rail fares came to an enormous £100 which must have been the equal of the top clubs. The club also paid out £74 in broken-time payments to players but it still managed to come out at the end of the season in the black for the first time in many years.

The 1898-99 season proved to be another struggle for the club in many ways. Only two league matches were won and, as a consequence, Morecambe faced once more the prospect of playing a test match to stay in the Senior Competition. In the cup it fared little better, losing to St Helens in the second round after two drawn games.

As Morecambe's miserable season drew to a close worse was to follow. The test match was against old rival Millom at Salford. This time Morecambe could not avoid relegation. It lost 3-11 and prepared to take its place in the Second Competition.

Two years were spent in the lower flight and the second of these proved the most successful. Morecambe ended the 1900-01 season as champions due largely to Birkenhead Wanderers' loss of form in its last few games. Consequently Morecambe had earned the right to play a test match to attempt to gain promotion. The team played Widnes, at Wigan's Springfield Park, on 20 April 1901. Widnes won 7-0 but the result proved to be academic as the second division was disbanded and the whole of the Northern Union restructured.

Morecambe found itself back in the Senior Competition in 1901-02 but found that nothing had changed on the playing field. The club managed only five wins and only avoided the wooden spoon by coming ahead of Altrincham and Radcliffe who had also come up from the Second Competition. At the end of the season the Northern Union was again reorganised and Morecambe now competed in the Second Division of the Northern Union. A new competition it may have been but the results on the field followed the same old pattern and supporters were now beginning to lose faith. The club played 34 league matches and won 9 but still could only finish one from bottom of the league with only Stockport below it.

Home attendances were declining steadily and the situation was not helped by the composition of teams in the league. Morecambe had only three home games against local sides Millom, Barrow and Lancaster and faced ten trips into Yorkshire and another to South Shields. Many of Morecambe's opponents were not considered to be attractive opposition and the club had to find increased expenses for railway fares on reduced gate money.

The heady days of profitability were now long gone. Travelling expenses saw to that and it was a struggle once more to make ends meet. The 1903-04 season saw Morecambe, which failed to win away, again finish one place off the bottom and it had to go cap in hand to the Northern Union for re-election, a mission safely accomplished. The following season saw a slight improvement with seven wins and two draws from 26 games but again only one club, on this occasion Bramley, separated Morecambe from the wooden spoon. With Birkenhead disbanding only Lancaster, Barrow, Millom and Rochdale Hornets provided opposition west of the Pennines and Morecambe had nine trips into Yorkshire. The three seasons of an inter-county, two division set-up had been a disaster for many clubs but especially for outposts such as Lancaster and Morecambe.

Lancaster threw in the towel but Morecambe struggled on to start one more season.

The league system had again been rearranged with a single league and positions to be decided by percentages. Club secretaries were free to arrange their own fixtures but any club not obtaining ten home and away games had to withdraw from the league.

Morecambe was again to be found in the lower reaches of the table finishing joint bottom with Brighouse Rangers. Only two wins, both at home against Normanton and Castleford, and four draws were achieved and a 0-8 defeat at Widnes on 21 April 1906 proved to be Morecambe's last game.

Matters came to a head at the end of the season. There can be little doubt that the senior clubs, reacting to the growing financial crisis in the game, realised the implications of their actions as they had already brought about the demise of some member clubs. They were not prepared to do anything about the situation and, as a result, another club and another area were lost to the professional game. The report of Morecambe's last AGM is shown and sums up the position the club was in and the isolation it must have felt.

The railway company reclaimed the land on which the playing pitch stood at a time when the club's finances were low. The Northern Union clubs would not give them fixtures simply because of Morecambe's low drawing power and the high cost of travelling to Morecambe. The Northern Union was not prepared to do anything at all to help them (as they had done nothing to help Lancaster the previous year).

Despite the perennial struggles on the pitch it was not a lack of playing success which brought about the club's demise. Debts were hardly a major reason either, totalling only £40. There was also a thriving junior rugby scene as witnessed by a report in the local Morecambe paper on 18 April 1906. A report of a local junior cup final quoted the presentation speech of Mr Deighton, from the Holme club. Although association was making some strides he thought the North Lancashire district, especially, was essentially a rugby district. Hardly a part of the world where rugby was in decline but the powers that be did not, or would not, see it that way and Morecambe went out of existence simply because other Northern Union clubs would not give it fixtures.

With the passing of the Morecambe club professional rugby disappeared and the game was lost to the Morecambe and Lancaster areas of the county.

Morecambe Visitor 29 August 1906

AFTER THIRTY YEARS
MORECAMBE RUGBY CLUB DISBANDED

Decision at the Annual Meeting

The annual meeting of the Morecambe Northern Union Football Club was held at the King's Arms on Thursday evening. Mr WJ Danee, chairman of the club, presided and supporting him were Messrs W Pyrah (treasurer), JW Coates (secretary), Messrs W Mayor, J Riley, Brown, Beach and several players.

The treasurer submitted the balance sheet which showed the deficit of the club to be £40. Reference was made to the fact that although the club had not finished very well in the league table they had nonetheless provided some good games. Regret was also felt respecting the fixtures which were not as numerous and as attractive as they might have been. A hope was expressed that the townspeople would rally round the club and help it continue considering its value to the town as an advertising medium. The report and balance sheet were approved.

The chairman, in the course of his remarks, said the club had never faced such difficulties as were in front of them this year....the unattractive fixture list which contained only ten league fixtures and the fact that the Midland Railway Company had given them notice to quit possession of the field, which of course necessitated the removal of the grandstand, securing another field and laying it out. That of course meant a big expense and where was the money coming from? It was a great pity for the club to discontinue and was a case of the big clubs swimming and the small clubs allowed to sink. Morecambe was not the first club to disband and would not be the last.

Mr J Riley suggested an emergency committee be formed to enquire the cost of removal and putting out a new field....to make enquiries as to what assistance they could get from the townspeople and report to a later meeting.

The Mayor said the large clubs had no sympathy for the smaller ones. After some discussion the chairman gave it as his opinion that, in view of the great difficulties faced, it was useless the club continuing as they would only run head-over-heels in debt. A resolution was moved and seconded that a committee be formed to interview the members of the town council and other townspeople to ascertain what funds could be raised towards the continuance of the club and report to a later meeting.

An amendment was moved and seconded that the club be disbanded and this was carried by nine votes to four. Mr Armstead said it was the Northern Union that had ruined them.

"They have", he continued, "no sympathy for us, they are all for themselves."

Radcliffe

FOUNDED: 1878
CEASED: 1903
REASON: financial problems
GROUND: Peel Park
HEADQUARTERS: Boar's Head Hotel
COLOURS: Amber and black

RADCLIFFE was one of the oldest rugby organisations in Lancashire. A local man, Mr Lawrence Ashworth, was the club's founder. The story goes that one day, tired of seeing a group of local lads loitering about, he bought them a ball and provided them with a field. "The founders of the Radcliffe Club" wrote the *Radcliffe Times* "were soon engaged in running in tries, dropping goals and scoring that relic of the past, the minor point."

At first the club had an association with the Close Wesleyan Sunday School but gradually went their own way. After playing on a field in Cross Lane a more suitable ground was found behind the Crown and Anchor Hotel.

In 1886 the Radcliffe club moved again and played at Withins to the north of the town. The headquarters was at the Forester's Arms kept by Mr and Mrs Paisley. The hostess took such a keen interest in the club's affairs that match reports often referred to Radcliffe as "Mrs Paisley's Boys."

It was during the time at Withins that Radcliffe enjoyed some of its most successful times culminating in victories in the South East Lancashire Cup finals of 1889 and 1890. One of the most prominent players was Tom Kent whose performances soon attracted the interest of some of the county's bigger clubs. In 1887 he "migrated" to Salford where he became a regular in the Lancashire side and earned England international honours. Kent was also a member of the first international side which toured Australia in 1888.

Kent retained his links with the Radcliffe club and on occasions returned to play for it. On 22 December 1888, Kent and a New Zealander, Joseph Warbrick, turned out for Radcliffe against Tyldesley, surely one of the first instances of a "Colonial" player playing for an English club. Warbrick was well known as the captain of the touring New Zealand Maori side and his appearance in the Radcliffe ranks attracted a great deal of interest.

Around this time Radcliffe was regarded as a rugby town despite having two soccer towns in Bury and Bolton in close proximity. "Since Radcliffe youths first learned to kick inflated leather, Rugby has been looked upon as the game to which they were devoted" commented the *Radcliffe Times*.

In 1890 Radcliffe left the Withins ground and took up residence at Peel Park in the centre of the town, sharing facilities with the

A Baines card from the 1890's featuring Radcliffe. (Photograph courtesy Robert Gate)

Radcliffe

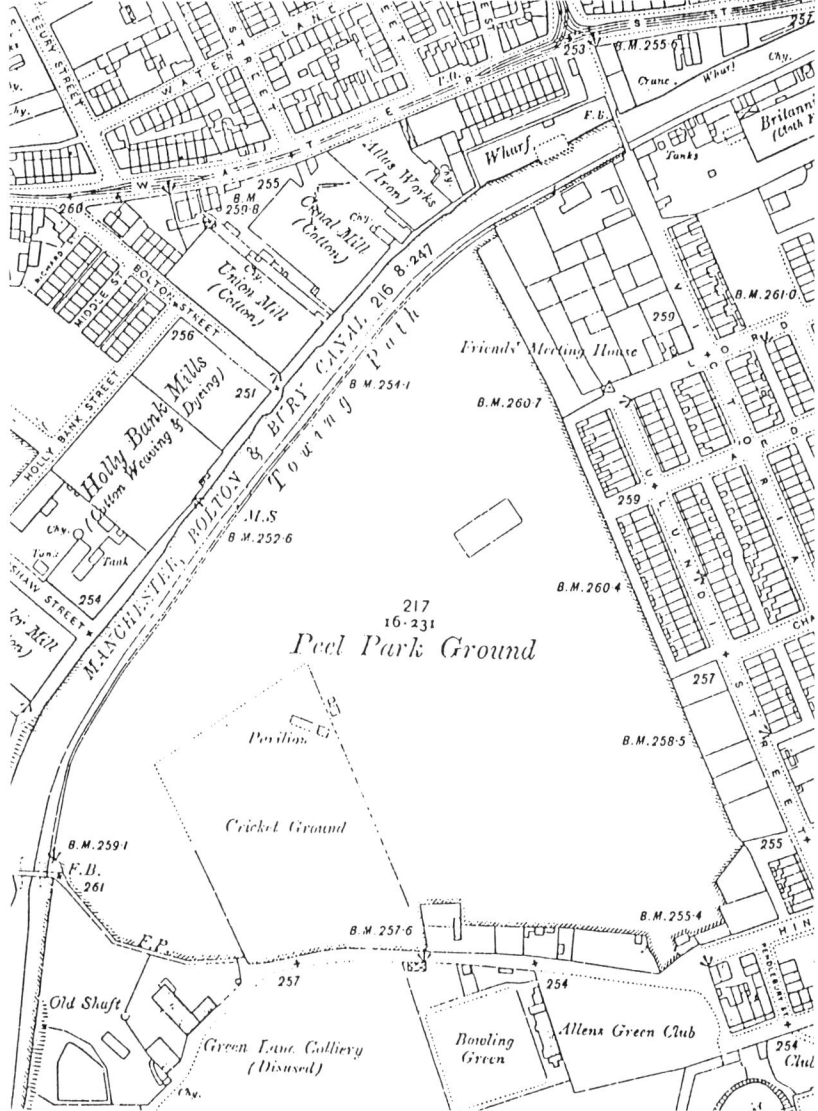

Peel Park, the home of the Radcliffe club. Bottom left shows the foot bridge across the canal, which may give a clue to the club's nickname, "The Bridgemen", (Reproduced from 1895 Ordnance Survey Map)

town cricket club.

The formation of a league system was looked upon with great anticipation in Radcliffe and seen as a way of rising through the ranks. In 1894-95 it was competing in the Third Competition before the events leading to the transfer of one of its players caused a near sensation. When Joe Smith, a goal-kicking three-quarter, joined Salford, Radcliffe objected to the Lancashire County officials over the nature of his transfer. As a result of its accusations Salford was suspended for professionalism and Smith banned from the game.

Salford responded in kind with allegations of its own over Radcliffe's efforts to persuade Smith to stay. The Lancashire County officials were suitably convinced and decided to also suspend the Radcliffe club which was struck out of the league for the season.

Radcliffe's officials were stoutly in favour of a continuance of the amateur regime but believed a player should receive compensation for loss of time when injured. The club was "promoted" to the Second Class Competition in 1895-96 due to the large number of gaps left by the defections to the Northern Union of the senior clubs.

Tom Kent returned to the club to play out his career and was appointed captain. Radcliffe's long-standing rival Tottington, which had merged with the Bury club, disbanded and many of the club's players and supporters transferred their allegiance to Radcliffe.

The destination of the championship came down to the final game of the season when Radcliffe went to Mossley on a Monday evening, 20 April 1896, needing to win to land the title. Mossley, who needed only to avoid defeat, held out for a pointless draw in front of a ground record crowd of around 3000.

This game proved to be Radcliffe's final one under the auspices of the Rugby Union. The great changes taking place in the game in the county left club officials with no choice but to join the Northern Union. The committee reported that "in all probability this was the last season of the league system in the Rugby

Tom Kent started and ended his illustrious career at Radcliffe. (Photograph courtesy Tim Auty)

Union" (in point of fact a league was played in 1896-97).

Radcliffe's first match under Northern Union rules was also a first for the newly-formed Castleford. Radcliffe travelled to open the Yorkshire club's ground and went down to a 0-9 defeat. The Radcliffe side was: Pearson; Clegg, Howarth, B Rouse, C Kent; G Rouse, Dowdall; Nightingale, Pollitt, Nixon, Sandiford, Booth, Buckley, Casey, Wallwork.

The 1896-97 season was to prove a frustrating one for clubs such as Radcliffe. Far from competing in a league system, it was left to organise a series of friendly games, its only competitive fixture being in the Challenge Cup at Wigan. Supported by "several hundred lusty shouters" Radcliffe acquitted itself well going down only to a first-half penalty goal by Wigan full-back Winstanley.

The first season of the Second Competition in 1897-98 was eagerly awaited and a crowd of 3000 saw the opening game against St Helens Recs. Radcliffe won 7-3, Wolfenden scoring a try and Smith and Holt kicking goals. Smith was now back in action, his suspension having finally been lifted.

Radcliffe gave a good account of itself being a match for all the teams apart from leaders Millom and Barrow and Peel Park was packed for some games, particularly the local derbies against Barton and Walkden. Radcliffe won nine of its last 13 league games to finish fourth.

In the Challenge Cup Radcliffe was due to play Hull at Peel Park but after an "almost unanimous" vote from the committee the decision was taken to accept Hull's offer to switch the tie. Radcliffe lost 0-18 but its guarantee of £130 was easily realised from a crowd of 10,000.

In 1898-99 a number of clubs banded together to form a South East Lancashire League to augment the Second Competition. Radcliffe lost only one league game and lifted the South East Lancashire Cup. In the Second Competition, Radcliffe played some attractive rugby at times with the veteran Smith and winger Benny Rouse the main try-getters. Sadly Radcliffe's long-standing rival Walkden folded during the season and Radcliffe's 32-0 win at the Stocks Enclosure proved to be Walkden's final game. This followed a 29-0 home win on New Year's Eve when Walkden's secretary wired to confirm that the match would definitely take place despite its inability to fulfil many of its fixtures.

Radcliffe took its place in the Border Towns League the following season, the competition replacing the South East Lancashire League. Though the season proved to be a most disappointing one, Radcliffe did run up the highest score in its history when it beat Hebden Bridge 52-0 with Smith scoring 5 tries and kicking 7 goals.

The competition aroused strong passions on 24 February 1900 when Radcliffe entertained Todmorden. A committee member of the visiting team, Mr Whitehead, refereed the game as the appointed official failed to turn up. A few minutes from the end he disallowed what would have been the winning try by Rouse. "The referee was struck by a Radcliffe player and spectators swarmed around him" reported the *Radcliffe Times*. The game was abandoned and Radcliffe was later ordered to pay compensation to Mr Whitehead and post warning notices around the ground.

An appeal for funds to continue the Border Towns League fell on deaf ears and in 1900-01 Radcliffe had only 16 league games and the cup ties to make ends meet. It was reported that Mr Fletcher, the owner of the Peel Park grounds, waived the rent for the year of £13 due to the club's financial difficulties.

A 4-3 home win over newly-relegated Tyldesley attracted one of the biggest crowds for a long time to Peel Park but a run of three successive defeats soon put an end to any hopes of promotion.

All but two of the league games had been played by the end of December and the

Benny Rouse was one of Radcliffe's most prominent players before being transferred to Wigan.

Radcliffe secretary searched desperately, and largely unavailingly, for opponents to play friendly games. Only Swinton obliged sending a near-full strength side to Peel Park. Radcliffe's season closed on 2 March when it went down 0-11 in the Challenge Cup at the hands of Leeds Parish Church.

Something had to be done if clubs such as Radcliffe were not to follow the likes of Barton and Walkden into oblivion. The Second Competition was formally disbanded and discussions took place throughout the summer, with a view to forming a Lancashire Senior Competition, fourteen clubs of Lancashire and Yorkshire having broken away to form their own Northern League.

To its dismay Radcliffe was excluded from the new set-up and the situation appeared bleak until Tyldesley's demise left a door open for Radcliffe to take its place in the Lancashire Senior Competition. The news was greeted with jubilation by rugby followers who had seen the growth in popularity of soccer gradually erode rugby's grip on the town. Bury was attracting gates of around 8000 for home games and created great interest with victory in the FA Cup Final of 1900, a feat repeated three years later.

The *Radcliffe Times*, which first appeared in the autumn of 1899, gave superb coverage of the Radcliffe club, far more than that afforded by its sister paper, the long-established *Bury Times*. Significantly, though, the match reports of Bury Football Club increased in size and Radcliffe's doings received fewer column inches as time went on.

"The association games flourished on congenial soil at Bury and its popularity soon spread to Radcliffe" remarked the *Radcliffe Times*. "Gradually the officials of the club which had dominated local football for years discovered that the new pastime was driving them out of the field....another blow was struck when the coal-getting industry practically left the town for it is well known that colliers are keen followers of the game."

The Radcliffe chairman attempted to rally support at the AGM in August 1901. "This season we will get visits from many of the prominent clubs who have not been to Radcliffe for years" he said. "If they do not attract the gates there is little point continuing." He called for support from the town "to stop the mass emigration to Gigg Lane."

The rugby club was not the only organisation in trouble as its co-tenants, Radcliffe Cricket Club, disbanded in 1898 and did not reform until 1906.

Far from being the catalyst for a change in fortunes, the 1901-02 season proved to be one long struggle for Radcliffe and for some of its fellow members of the now defunct Lancashire Second Competition. To make matters worse Radcliffe had two league points deducted for making an illegal approach to an Oldham player.

The indecision over the summer had hindered the recruitment of players but it was felt that the committee had assembled a reasonable side. A 13-2 home win over Altrincham raised hopes but it soon became clear that Radcliffe was struggling to be competitive against the better sides.

Radcliffe suffered some heavy away defeats, 2-47 to Barrow, 0-41 to Lancaster, 0-41 to Rochdale Hornets, 0-40 to Widnes and 0-71 to Hull KR and the club was frequently unable to put out its strongest side due to a lack of funds for broken-time.

The situation was exacerbated by poor weather which led to the postponement of a number of home games. In desperation, when the pitch for the game with Barrow on 21 December was unfit due to water and ice, the committee erected the posts in an adjoining field which was "barely playable." The game failed to finish when fog came down and the receipts were under £1. Radcliffe finished the season with a run of six home fixtures but, by this time, morale was low and the crowds numbered only a few hundred.

A home defeat in the Challenge Cup by Goole was a significant financial blow and Radcliffe was reported to the Northern Union for failing to forward its opponent's share of the gate receipts. Finally Radcliffe recorded its second win of the season defeating Morecambe 4-3 with the aid of two goals by Smith. The side now largely comprised local youngsters, who were praised for their pluck and courage, in the face of tremendous odds.

Radcliffe could raise only eleven men for the home clash with eventual champions Wigan, but went down only 0-16, and closed the campaign with a 7-23 defeat at home to Barrow.

This match, played on 19 April 1902, was to prove the final game in Radcliffe's history and the *Radcliffe Times* reported "The attendance on Saturday was a fair reflection of the interest at present taken in the Rugby game. It was very small indeed and when the referee's expenses were paid Barrow found that they had made the long journey at some financial loss."

Radcliffe applied for membership of the new second division of the Northern Union but as the *Radcliffe Times* reported "at a protracted meeting....Radcliffe's application was refused, a proceeding which is certainly calculated to discourage the club's most ardent supporters."

It was originally intended to keep the club going by playing a few friendly games during the 1902-03 season but no games were played and the club was formally wound up early in 1903.

In 1902-03 Radcliffe Rangers, formed in 1901, carried the rugby flag in the town, competing in the Manchester League. In its first season Rangers had shared the Peel Park ground but now the club moved to a new field off Stand Lane.

Peel Park was taken over by the Manchester Welsh Rugby Union side, which moved from Old Trafford, in 1903. The arrangements were overseen by a solicitor and former Radcliffe player and committee member, Bowen Evans, who had joined the club when Fleetwood folded.

Radcliffe Rangers recruited many of the old Radcliffe players and enjoyed some successful seasons in the amateur ranks. In March 1907 the club reached the first round of the Challenge Cup losing 0-13 at home to York. Despite poor weather and a counter-attraction at Gigg Lane a crowd of 1400 realised receipts of £25. The crowd figure, though, was a one-off. The *Radcliffe Times* commented that "Rangers are the strongest side for miles around yet receive poor support."

St Helens Recs

FOUNDED: 1879
CEASED: 1898
REASON: financial problems
GROUND: Boundary Road
HEADQUARTERS: Talbot Hotel
COLOURS: Maroon jersey with green collar, dark blue shorts, black stockings

ST HELENS Recreation, having decided to join the Northern Union, was a natural choice for inclusion in the Second Competition in its inaugural season. Far from leading to a bright new chapter in the club's history, however, Recs' season became a tale of woe and the famous old club failed to see out the campaign.

Formed as a sports section of Pilkington Brothers Glass Works, Recs played at Boundary Road, a ground first used by the St Helens club. Recs supplied a number of players to the Lancashire county side including a forward, Jimmy Pyke, who won England international honours against Wales in 1892. Pyke together with another Recs forward, P Fildes, had played for Lancashire in the 1890-91 season when they won the County Championship for the first time.

Recs joined the West Lancashire Union and competed in the West Lancashire and Border Towns Cup in its inaugural season, 1885-86, reaching the semi-finals where the team lost to Aspull after a replay. Two years later a ground record was set when 10,000 saw Recs lose to Wigan in the same competition. The *Wigan Examiner* reported that many spectators had bet a week's wages on the result. Not surprisingly it was stated that "there were very few cool heads about the place."

Recs also competed in the Rugby Union Lancashire Club Championship in its first season, 1892-93, finishing a creditable fifth. The decision was then taken to bow out of competitive games. It was felt that the strong passions aroused by such fixtures were contrary to the philosophies of the club. Thereafter Recs decided to play friendly games only.

Despite declining to take part in the Club Championship which, from 1893 onwards, was extended to three divisions, Recs still maintained their reputation as one of the leading sides in the county.

In 1895 Recs remained stoutly loyal to the Rugby Union despite St Helens' switch to Northern Union. The *St Helens Reporter*, after commenting on the events leading up to the breakaway, carried the news that "the Recs club remain faithful to the English Union and look forward to supplying Lancashire with half-a-dozen county players during the season." This prediction was spot-on for six Recs players, Crossley, Traynor, Briers, Mousdale, Pilkington and Seddon featured in Lancashire selections in the 1895-96 season.

Judged in isolation the decision was a reasonable one. The problem was that the clamour of clubs to join the new Union was such that Recs' fixture options rapidly depleted. Recs' original fixture list for the 1895-96 season included games against the likes of Wigan, Leigh, Tyldesley, Warrington, Broughton Rangers, Runcorn and Bradford all of which had resigned from the Rugby Union.

Recs was left to pick up the pieces with remaining fixtures against teams such as Swinton, New Brighton, Birkenhead Wanderers, Morecambe, Pemberton, Liverpool, Liverpool Old Boys and Altrincham. As, by the end of the 1895-96 season, many of those clubs had either decided to join the Northern Union or were in the process of deciding to join, Recs' projected fixture list for the following season had plenty of open dates.

THE RUGBY LEAGUE MYTH

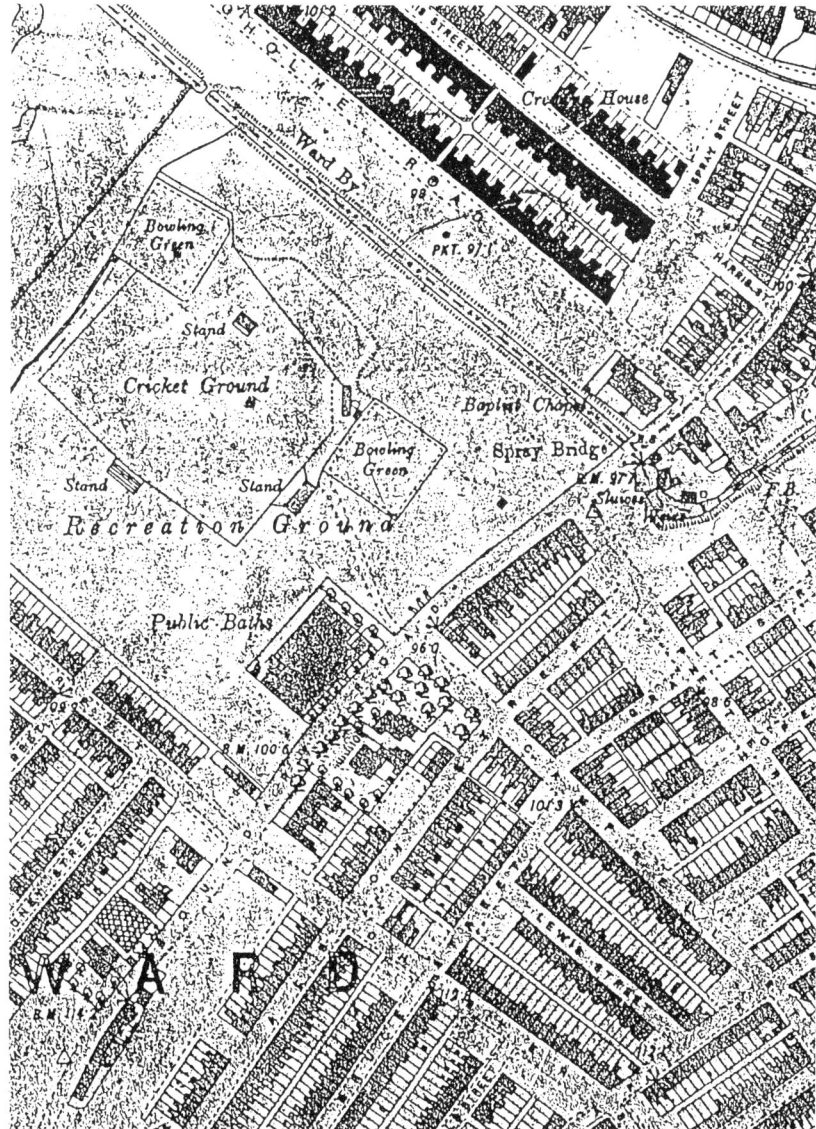

St Helens Recs shared the Boundary Road ground with the cricket club. (Reproduced from 1893 Ordnance Survey Map)

Recs' decision to steer clear of competitive games was rebounding on the club. "Undoubtedly something had to be done to rescue the club from oblivion....spectators do not want to see friendly games" commented the *St Helens Advertiser*. The decision even to continue playing rugby had been in the balance and, if the decision to switch to Northern Union had not been ratified, the club would in all likelihood have folded. It was decided at a meeting held on 13 April 1896 to resign from membership of the Lancashire and English Rugby Union and apply for membership of the Northern Union. "Secretary Mr Wilfred Ellison has accordingly carried out this instruction" reported the local press.

Recs' first game under the Northern Union was a hastily-arranged friendly against Crompton, at Boundary Road, on 25 April 1896. A drop-goal by Appleton gave Recs a 4-3 win. The home side lined up as follows: R Seddon; Hope, Traynor, Appleton, McLees; Pennington, Allen; Mousdale, Dolan, Chapman, Barnett, Sidler, Burrows, Wilson, Turner.

In 1896-97 Recs suffered from the delay in forming a feeder league to the Lancashire Senior Competition. Much of the impetus behind the switch was lost as the Recs club was forced to arrange a whole series of friendly games, many of them against the senior clubs when they both had blank dates. Recs' only competitive fixture was in the Challenge Cup when, after a first round bye, it accepted Rochdale Hornets' offer to switch the tie for a cash guarantee. Even so Recs was confident of victory but hopes proved unfounded as Hornets ran out 8-0 winners.

For clubs such as Recs the formation of the Lancashire Second Competition came a season too late as many of Recs' followers had drifted away. In the early stages of the 1896-97 season gates had been promising, 5000, for example, seeing Recs defeat Crompton in September. By the season's end, however, gates were severely reduced as spectators tired of seeing the same opponents for the second or even third time. The spectators were now geared up to the system of league tables and cared little for non-competitive games.

The whole future of the rugby club was up for discussion and, if Recs had not been admitted to the Second Competition in the summer of 1897, the club would have closed down. There was a move to form an association club instead of the rugby team but, after much internal wrangling, a compromise was reached.

Recs would compete in the Lancashire Second Competition and a newly-formed Recs association club would compete in the Lancashire Alliance. As best they could, the two sections arranged fixtures so there would not be a clash of home dates. If this was the case the soccer side would play ay the City Road ground with the rugby code continuing at Boundary Road.

There were a number of changes in the side for Recs' opening league game. The club had acquired two Welsh three-quarters, DH Edmonds and FA Llewellyn, from Newport and A Siddall, a centre, from Rochdale Hornets. Recs lost the first two games 3-7 to Radcliffe and 0-3 to Barton and found that enthusiasm for the first home league game was waning. The two Welsh players soon departed the scene. "Their interests lie in some other area" was the official line.

The soccer club had made a good start and was attracting a good level of support, and a crowd of 2000, considerably down on the soccer club's gates, saw Recs defeat Altrincham 11-0. Recs then had a fine 5-3 win over Millom before losing 6-15 at home to Barrow.

The next game was at home to Lancaster and a crowd described as "meagre" saw Recs win 10-3. "Everyone had gone to Prescot to see the association match" was the explanation in the local press. The geographical spread of sides in the Second Competition was such that, only with a fair degree of latitude, could any of the games be described as "local derbies". The soccer club, on the other hand, played in a league where most of the sides were in close proximity to each other and so spectators could easily follow their side away.

The situation was brought home clearly for Recs' next home game against Crompton. "Instead of the 6000 who the week before had cheered on the association team there were less than 1500" was the local reporter's estimate. The irony was that Recs was now adapting well to life in the new league and were becoming a side to be reckoned with.

Successive home wins over two of the leading sides, Barton and Millom, just before Christmas and a victory at Fleetwood and draw at Birkenhead stretched Recs' unbeaten run to eight games and established the club as one of the challengers for the championship. In friendly games against the senior clubs Recs also acquitted itself well.

Despite this there was little interest from the townsfolk in its affairs and for the first home game of the New Year, against Radcliffe, there was a crowd of only a few hundred to see Recs win 10-3. Reports on home games frequently referred to a "lamentable dearth of spectators." Long trips to Lancaster and Ulverston stretched the club's finances and the situation was becoming desperate. Payments for broken-time had to be found from somewhere and the rugby section could only survive for a limited period unless something was done.

Meanwhile the soccer section was flourishing and the contrasting fortunes of the two clubs were reflected on Saturday 5 March. Recs played Ulverston at home, recording an eighth win in nine home league games with a late drop-goal from Crossley. The attendance was very poor as the soccer side was also at home, playing Darwen Olympic in the semi-final of the Lancashire Junior Cup and a crowd of 8000 saw them win 4-1.

Recs played one more game, fulfilling a friendly engagement at Hull KR, going down 5-22 before the inevitable news of the club's demise. The *St Helens Reporter* of 25 March 1898 issued the following statement. "Last Monday at a meeting of the committee of the Recreation football sections, a very important step was taken. It was reported that the ground in Boundary Road had been so much cut up by the playing of football that if it was further used for that purpose the Recs Cricket Club would be unable to have the ground ready for the start of the cricket season."

It was resolved to play the remaining association games on the City Road ground and, as all but two of the remaining rugby games were to be played away, it was decided to disband the rugby team. It was stated that, with the exception of friendlies at Halifax and Hull KR, where Recs accepted a guarantee, there had been a "distinct loss" on every rugby game played during the season.

The meeting concluded that "henceforth the Recreation club will solely confine its attentions to the association game which has been so well supported during the present season."

Interest in rugby it was stated had "waned considerably" despite the club's good playing record. "The Recs club can look back to successes which made it talked about in the whole of the north of England....in the days when the club attracted large gates" concluded the report.

The Recs club was far from alone in having financial problems and a telling comment was made that the decision should help the St Helens club to "replenish its coffers." Recs, which had completed 18 league fixtures, became the second club, following Crompton, to disband during the season. The decision was hardly met with approval coming as late in the campaign as it did.

Barrow was particularly incensed as its rival for the championship Millom, which had lost both home and away against Recs, would now have those defeats struck out of the amended league table. Barrow was also denied a home gate from Recs' visit.

At the time Recs was lying third in the league with 11 wins, 2 draws and 5 defeats. The club was only two points behind leaders Millom and had a game in hand, though second placed Barrow had 25 points from 16 games.

Unlike other clubs which had a dragon-fly existence in the Northern Union, Recs was not lost to the game in the long-term. In June

1913 it made a successful application to rejoin the Northern Union and played in the Lancashire Combination. The home ground was now at City Road.

Recs was admitted as a senior member of the Northern Union in January 1919 when competitive games resumed following the end of World War One. Recs' membership ceased in 1939 when it resigned from the Rugby League due to financial reasons. The club was reformed on amateur lines after the Second World War.

Tyldesley

FOUNDED: 1879
CEASED: 1901
REASON: financial problems
GROUND: Well Street
HEADQUARTERS: George and Dragon Hotel
COLOURS: White jerseys, blue shorts

TYLDESLEY achieved fame and a certain amount of prosperity through some stirring deeds in the late 1880's and 1890's before a combination of damaging factors brought about a sudden and unexpected fall from prominence. Tyldesley's only season as a Second Competition club, in 1900-01, was to be its last.

A man who later became one of Tyldesley's most prominent and longest-serving players, Fred Shaw, founded the club. The first headquarters were just outside the village at Garrett Hall. Tyldesley's players were described as "mainly of working-class origins....in good trim and, due to the nature of their handicraft, as hard as nails."

In 1881 a more accessible ground was taken at Sale Lane and the club steadily increased its prestige. An occasional playing member, Frank Wright, who chiefly assisted the Manchester club gained an England cap in 1881.

Tyldesley's great local adversary was Leigh and the two sides began a strong and largely healthy rivalry, with games between the two clubs frequently attracting gates of between three and four thousand.

In 1886 Tyldesley moved again to an enclosure backing on to the cricket ground at Well Street situated at the bottom of the hill leading up to the main part of the village. This gave an opportunity to develop good facilities, a grandstand was constructed, and other improvements carried out.

The *Wigan Examiner* graphically described Wigan's visit in January 1888: "Wigan explored the barbaric regions of prehistoric Lancashire or "Tinsley Bongs" as the semi-pastoral region of Lancashire is referred to by the natives. It is a village where the houses seem creeping up slopes....in the midst of the cotton spinning institutions and mines there is a devouring appetite for football food."

Tyldesley's rise can be largely attributed to the acquisition of a famous half-back, Buff Berry, in the 1887-88 season. Formerly of the famous Kendal Hornets club the Westmorland county player was one of many players from Kendal who tried their luck with Lancashire clubs.

Berry was enticed to join the *Bongers*, as Tyldesley was known, by the offer of more regular employment. Contemporary reports suggest there was more than one or two "back handers" flying around in what was supposed to be a strictly amateur game with Tyldesley being far from the worst culprits.

Whatever the circumstances surrounding Berry's arrival his appearance in the white Tyldesley jersey had an immediate effect. Already famed for the strength and size of the club pack, Berry's skills completed the jigsaw. Described as "burly and muscular with a tremendous pair of hands, a good kicker and passer, though the reverse of speedy" Berry brought the best out of those around him and forged himself a formidable reputation.

In his first season at the club Tyldesley carried off a major honour, lifting the West Lancashire Cup in its third season of operation, by defeating Widnes before a crowd of 10000 at Warrington. Tyldesley forward Joe Hodkinson scored the game's only try converted by Shaw.

Tyldesley's Well Street ground was in close proximity to the cricket ground. The present Tyldesley RUFC play on the same site. (Reproduced from 1893 Ordnance Survey Map)

"Tyldesley had their day and a night of it if the record of beer sold is any criterion" reported The Athletic News. Tyldesley's methods did not, however, win universal approval. After the semi-final win over Wigan the Wigan Examiner reported that "their offside tactics and questionable tackling led to an undesirable feeling in sections of the crowd." All of which mattered little to Berry and his adoring public.

Berry "practically coached the whole of the players and the locals showed a wonderful improvement after he had been with them a short time" reported the Leigh Journal.

Buff Berry's feats were now well known far outside the locality and in the 1890-91 season he was chosen to play in each of England's three international games. He also played in all the fixtures for Lancashire which won the Rugby Union County Championship for the first time.

Buff was joined by his brother Billy and together they forged a formidable half-back partnership behind a pack which acquired something of a notorious reputation for its sturdiness. Two members, George Woodward and James Shepherd, won county honours and the former played for the North. The locals felt he deserved England honours but it was reported that his play was "of too rough-spun a character to suit the lady-like Southerners."

Despite a consistently good playing record Tyldesley was regarded as an unfashionable outfit and it was something of a surprise when the invitation came to join the First Class ranks of the Lancashire Club Championship in its inaugural season 1892-93. The Bongers justified inclusion by finishing in third place.

Two years later in a momentous season for the game in Lancashire, Tyldesley won the championship, the last before the breakaway though the triumph was diluted by the fact that three clubs, Salford, Leigh and Wigan were thrown out of the competition during the season for breaches of the laws relating to professionalism. A ground record crowd of 7000, which realised receipts of over £100, saw Tyldesley clinch the title with victory over St Helens.

The growing discontent among the senior clubs of Lancashire and Yorkshire ensured that this would be the last season for many of them in the Rugby Union ranks and Tyldesley became one of the founder members of the Northern Union competing with distinction in the 1895-96 season. Despite the demands of a hastily-arranged 42 game programme Tyldesley finished sixth confirming its ranking among the top clubs in the North.

The following season, 1896-97, saw the formation of two county leagues to replace the one division set-up and Tyldesley finished third in the Lancashire Senior Competition and reached the last eight of the Challenge Cup. Tyldesley, regarded among the game's

Buff Berry (left) and his brother Billy (right),formed a formidable half-back combination for Tyldesley. Buff also played for Barton while Billy turned out for Walkden. (Photograph courtesy Alf Yates)

Tyldesley captain Fred Shaw holds the West Lancashire Cup following his side's victory in 1888. (Photograph courtesy Alf Yates)

elite, suffered a fall from grace which was sudden and from which it never recovered.

Tyldesley had always been regarded as a small club which lacked the financial clout of many of its rivals. The onset of out-and-out professionalism inevitably damaged clubs with limited resources. Moreover the rules of the game were also changing as the Northern Union executive sought to make the game more attractive.

Tyldesley's great strength had always been in the forwards and the rule changes, which sought to reduce the amount of forward play and scrummages and increase back play and passing movements, reduced their effectiveness. From all accounts Tyldesley failed to adapt to the rule changes and were constantly criticised for following crude and old-fashioned methods.

The financial problems also surfaced and the Berry brothers were tempted away. Buff joined Second Competition side Barton, the financial inducements being far greater than he was offered by Tyldesley, while Billy moved to Walkden.

Failing to win away Tyldesley finished third-bottom of the league and, to make matters worse, the ground was closed down by the authorities for a few weeks after the referee was mobbed by home supporters following a home cup-tie defeat at the hands of Broughton Rangers.

The following season, 1898-99, was again a struggle with the committee having to dig deep into its own pockets to fund away trips. Tyldesley at least avoided the dreaded bottom spot which would have meant having to justify first-class placing by playing the Second Competition champions in a test match. Crowds were disappointing, numbering only a few hundred on occasions, and the lack of support meant that expenses had to be cut back to a minimum.

At the AGM of 1899 it was reported that the club's debts now totalled £198. Gate receipts for the season amounted to £326 but broken-time and travelling expenses alone accounted for £266.

In 1899-1900 Tyldesley's day of reckoning finally came when the club finished bottom of the table with only five points. The forwards were still a sturdy set, with the veteran

Woodward continuing to be a stalwart member of the pack, but the team was constantly outclassed when it came to open play. The test match saw Tyldesley lose its senior status by going down 8-22 to Barrow at Lancaster. It was a disappointingly listless performance by the *Bongers*.

Tyldesley began life in the Second Competition with hopes of regaining senior status but it soon became clear that such ambitions were illusory. Crowds sunk to a few hundred and there was such a severe lack of funds for broken-time that players were often forced to play for nothing. As a result many stayed away and Tyldesley officials were constantly having to desperately search around the amateur ranks for players to make up the numbers.

Buff Berry reappeared in a number of games and Woodward completed his twentieth playing season but there were few bright spots in a disastrous campaign.

Financial problems were mounting and before the final home game of the season, against Birkenhead Wanderers on 6 April 1901, bailiffs took control of the turnstiles on behalf of the Inland Revenue authorities. A crowd of 400 saw Tyldesley, forced to field a team half-full of local juniors due to selected players not turning up, give a surprisingly resilient performance. They won 9-2 with tries by Madeley (2) and Bancroft and in doing so dealt an enormous blow to the visitor's championship hopes.

A few days later Tyldesley's days were ended when, due to mounting debts, various club effects were sold at auction for £30 under a distraint for rent and unpaid income tax.

Ironically if Tyldesley had managed to hang on there might have been a way back to senior ranks. The decision of 14 Lancashire and Yorkshire clubs to form their own Northern League, in time for the start of the 1901-02 season, meant there were spaces to be filled in the Lancashire Senior Competition. The county officials left a place vacant for Tyldesley until it became clear that the club would not be revived and, eventually, Radcliffe was allocated Tyldesley's position at a meeting held in Manchester on 23 July 1901.

If Tyldesley had survived it might only have been a brief respite for small clubs, with limited resources, were finding it increasingly difficult to compete in the Northern Union. Commenting on the steady deterioration which finally culminated in Tyldesley's demise the *Leigh Journal* had strong feelings where the reasons lay. When the Northern Union was founded, it stated, the "ostensible object of the founders....was to legalise payments to players for broken-time". It soon became clear that the outcome of this would be "open and undiluted professionalism."

Even though there was "not the slightest doubt" that payments to crack players had been made before 1895 the practice now became "general and undisguised, and many leading clubs of the two counties were soon engaged in a fierce and costly competition for the services of well-known players. The inevitable result of this was to cripple and finally crush out of all existence the football organisations in relatively small centres.

"Smaller organisations who had to rely largely on local talent were unable to hold their own against the powerful battalions which were arrayed against them." The team, especially in the backs, was weakened and players who had previously given good service retired from playing or left to join other clubs. "A series of reverses in the field caused the players to lose heart and confidence, the gates steadily declined....and the downward trend was gradual but sure" concluded the report.

The amateur game continued to flourish in the town and Well Street's future was secured when the ground's owner, a local coal mine owner, William Ramsden, passed the ground over to the Tyldesley Rugby Union side formed just before the First World War. The side still play at Well Street and a visit there is a rewarding one for looking around the playing area it is easy to imagine the days when Tyldesley, the *"burly Bongers"*, were a force in the game.

Ulverston

FOUNDED: 1882
CEASED: 1900
REASON: reverted to amateur ranks
GROUND: Morecambe Road
HEADQUARTERS: Grapes Hotel
COLOURS: White jerseys, blue shorts

At the time of the formation of the Northern Union the Ulverston club was enjoying the most successful spell in its short history. A seaport and market town on Morecambe Bay, Ulverston had a station on the LMS Railway and was the centre of a mining district, an industry whose workers were traditional supporters of the rugby game.

Ulverston played at the Fitzbridge ground which was often referred to as the Morecambe Road enclosure. Reports suggest that the ground was little more than a roped-off field. Games against neighbouring teams such as Barrow, Dalton, Askam and Millom aroused great enthusiasm in the town and matches were played against teams from farther afield as the club built up its reputation.

From the early days the town's geographical location meant that in order to fulfil a testing fixture list the club had to be prepared to travel considerable distances and also persuade clubs from Lancashire and Yorkshire to travel to Ulverston.

The club's first venture into a competitive league structure outside of the largely parochial North-Western League, was in 1893-94 when it finished third, behind promoted St Helens and Leigh, in the Lancashire Club Championship (Second Class).

Elevation to the top rank was not long in coming, for in the summer of 1895, the large number of clubs joining the Northern Union left gaps to fill in the first-class ranks. Ulverston was promoted as one of the clubs to replace the defectors and enjoyed a highly successful season finishing "runners-up" to champions Morecambe. Forward R Forshaw, half-back W McDonald and centre R Lewis all won Lancashire county honours while H Wilson and J Jackson played for Westmorland.

The following season Ulverston decided against continuing in the Lancashire league set-up and competed solely in the North-Western League. However, links with the Lancashire County Rugby Union were maintained and Ulverston became the first winner of the Lancashire Cup which now operated on a knock-out system.

The final against Castleton Moor was played at Lancaster on 10 April 1896, Ulverston running out a convincing winner 21-0. Forshaw scored two tries and Wilson, Hine and Lewis one each whilst Hine also kicked three goals. The victorious Ulverston side was: Murphy; Wilson, Lewis, Hine, Newsham; Hall, McDonald; Jackson, Whittle, Forshaw, McNicholas, Turner, Clements, Ireland, Backhouse.

An excited crowd gathered at the railway station as Ulverston's players arrived home with the cup. The team was drawn through the packed street on a four horse charabanc preceded by the Volunteer Band.

The decision to join the Northern Union was not taken lightly but with all the rival clubs having decided, or being on the verge of changing, Ulverston went with the tide. At a special meeting held at the Central Hall the unanimous decision was taken to join the Northern Union.

Ulverston was a founder member of the Lancashire Second Competition and enjoyed a successful first season ending third behind

Ulverston

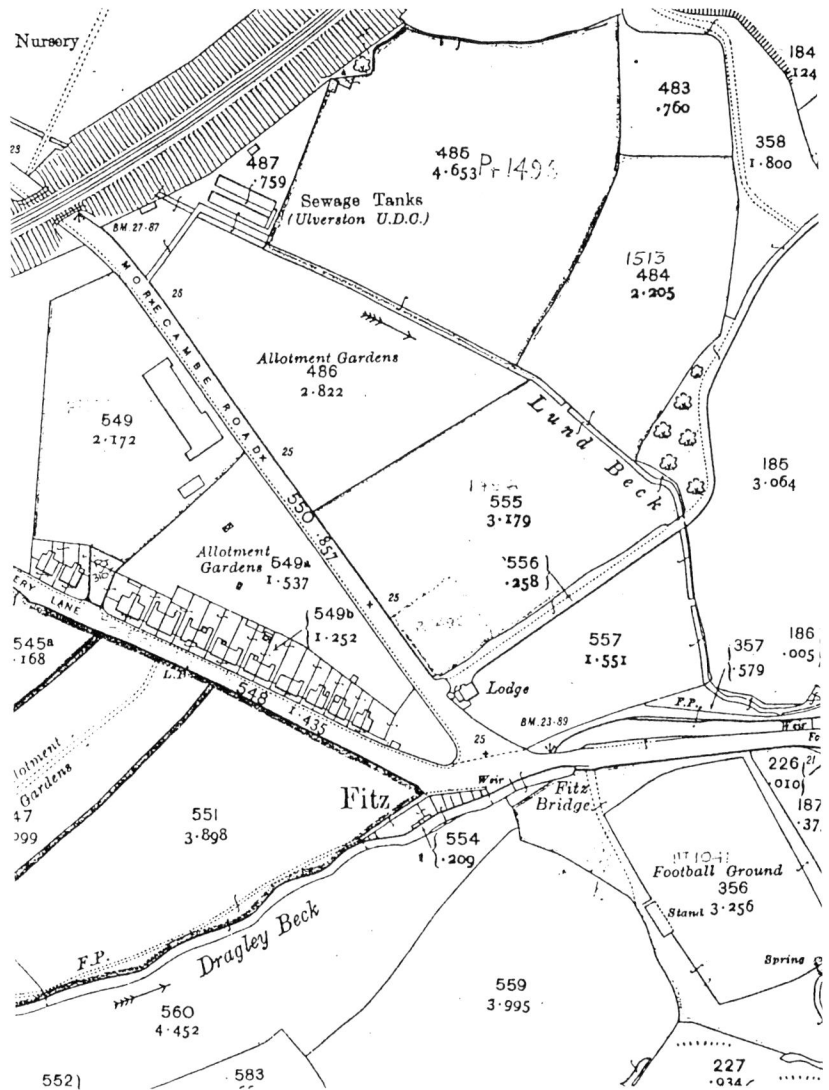

The Ulverston club ground. Locally, it was referred to as the Fitzbridge ground after the nearby bridge, but the local newspaper of the day always referred to it as the Morecambe Road enclosure. The present Ulverston ARLFC ground is only a couple of fields away from the old ground. (Reproduced from 1897 Ordnance Survey Map)

An Ulverston team group from the 1895-86 season.
Back row: J Whittle, W Hadwin, J McNicholas, J Shaw, R Casson (Sec.), J Jackson, R Forshaw, F Moran, H Wilson. **Middle row:** W Turner, J Jackson, J R Robinson (Capt.), W McDonald, F W Poole, **Front row:** W Hine, W Hall, J Jenkinson.
(Photograph courtesy Jim Heyes)

joint leaders Millom and Barrow. The club also competed again in the North-Western League, some of the games counting in both league tables. Ulverston's first game under Northern Union rules was a NWL fixture at home to Dalton on 11 September 1897. Lewis and Forshaw scored tries in a 6-5 win.

The following Saturday a crowd of 2000 saw Ulverston's first game in the Lancashire Second Competition when Barrow drew 0-0 at the Morecambe Road Enclosure. The Ulverston side was: Murphy; Platt, Lewis, Robinson, Forshaw; Hall, McDonald; Jackson, Whittle, Duke, Elliott, Fell, Stainton, Clements, Porter. Admission prices had been raised due, stated the Ulverston committee, "to so many big railway journeys."

Apart from a 36-5 home win over Fleetwood, most of the matches were low-scoring affairs. The games against Barrow and Millom attracted good home crowds and helped finance the number of long and expensive trips to south Lancashire and Cheshire. Six successive away league games at Altrincham, Fleetwood, Crompton, Birkenhead, Lancaster and Radcliffe hardly helped the cash-flow and it was soon a struggle to keep the club's finances on an even keel.

It was also difficult to keep the best players at the club and, among others, Forshaw left for Hull, Lewis for Leeds Parish Church, Murphy was enticed to join Barrow and Hall joined Lancaster. The players who stayed were rumoured to be discontented with their terms and refused to turn out for the Christmas Day game at Barrow. "Their behaviour has done no little harm" concluded the *Barrow News*.

Long trips also caused problems in organisation and when Ulverston got to Radcliffe on 8 January it was found to the team's horror that the hamper containing the playing strip had been left behind. Ulverston "turned out in various coloured costumes much to the amusement of the spectators" described a local reporter.

Despite relative playing success home crowds were disappointing. A home tie in the Challenge Cup competition was seen as a financial lifeline but, as the *Ulverston Advertiser* remarked, "even the visit of the well-known Runcorn side failed to arouse any enthusiasm in the town." The visitors won comfortably 19-2.

The AGM reported a reasonably optimistic picture as gate receipts for the season totalled £284, an increase of £148 on the previous campaign. Broken-time payments were £67 and railway fares £130 and the club ended the season with £61 in hand. A local junior club, Ulverston Parish Church, had been formed and this outfit effectively served as the senior club's A team.

By the following season, 1898-99, some of the initial enthusiasm for the new competition was visibly waning despite some good wins in the league. Travel problems were also increasing. Ulverston was due to play at Altrincham on 7 January 1899 but the game was postponed due to a frozen pitch. The hosts had been unable to alert Ulverston in time and a needless expense was incurred to Ulverston's obvious displeasure. As a result Ulverston refused to fulfil the fixture.

Ulverston also refused to make the journey to Barton on 3 December 1898 as the Manchester club refused to give a guarantee that it would play the return. For similar reasons Ulverston did not play at Walkden on 11 February 1899. In each case it was stated that the costs of railway fares would total £12, an expense not to be incurred lightly, if there was little likelihood of recouping it by way of a home gate. Ulverston's suspicions proved well founded as both clubs failed to see out the season.

To place the amount in context Ulverston's best home gate was only £19 for the visit of Barrow in February. Many home attendances failed to meet the expenses and even the visit of the touring Halifax side over Easter failed to attract anything like a reasonable turn-out.

In the circumstances Ulverston did remarkably well to finish fourth. Full-back Fred Moran was the best player but, inevitably, he joined the exodus being tempted to join Fleetwood.

The arrival of neighbouring Dalton in 1899-1900 hardly helped Ulverston's growing despair even though Ulverston secured a 3-0 home win over the newcomers on 21 October in "one of the most fierce contests ever fought on the Morecambe Road Enclosure" and completed a double when Whittle's try decided the return game at Dalton three weeks later.

At this stage of the season Ulverston had won four of the opening seven games, another being drawn, but fortunes soon began to turn for the worse. The lack of funds to pay broken-time and the long railway journeys to away games worsened the club's financial situation and home gates were very disappointing. The club was only able to see out the season thanks to a £30 gift from a supporter. Players' terms were reduced and the A team disbanded as an economy measure.

Player discontent was rife and some refused to turn out, especially for long away trips. Reports also suggested that many of those who did play were far from at the peak of physical fitness. Ulverston made the journey to Lancaster with only eleven players and committee men made up the numbers. One un-named player, who had refused to play, proceeded to shout insults from the sidelines throughout the game and was "much the worse for drink."

Ulverston lost eleven of its last twelve league games, scoring only four tries in the process and conceding 125 points, its only success being a 6-0 home win over Radcliffe on 10 March 1900 when Lloyd scored two tries. Ulverston's last game of the season, and last as a professional club, was against Altrincham on Monday 16 April 1900 when the visitors won 6-0. "There was a very thin attendance" reported the *Barrow News* "and one hears rumours that the club is to be wound up."

The club's situation was described as "desperate". Football prospects under the Northern Union "are as dead as a door nail" the report continued. "The committee have had enough and a chain horse would not draw some of them into office again."

A General Meeting was held in the town on 31 August 1900, to discuss the financial position and the organisation of a purely amateur side. The treasurer, Mr Harrison, stated that gate receipts for the 1899-1900 season had totalled £146 and subscriptions amounted to a further £17. Total expenses for the season were £252. Outstanding debts were now over £110. It was a situation which clearly could not continue.

The committee had decided enough was enough and did not want to incur any additional liabilities. In view of the debts there was no chance of continuing as a professional team. As the club owned the field there was no reason why it could not continue in an amateur capacity of some sort.

The majority of players offered their services free of cost and promised to play for railway fares only. An association club was also formed to play home fixtures on alternate weeks at the ground. "Prospects are now much brighter" was the more optimistic tone being reported. As a result of these decisions the rugby game was to continue in the town with the Ulverston club now functioning on an entirely amateur basis.

For the 1900-01 season Ulverston was to compete in the North-West Junior League alongside Askam, Dalton, Barrow St George's, Barrow St James, Roose, Leven Valley, Haverigg and the reserve teams of Millom and Barrow. Ulverston also joined a Westmorland and North Lancashire League competition. Teams in this league comprised Kirkby Lonsdale, Morecambe Parish Church, Holme, Kendal Hornets and Lancaster A.

"We are, after all, to have a team in Ulverston" concluded the *Ulverston Advertiser*. "The committee are making every effort and there is no reason why an amateur side cannot compete successfully."

These proved to be prophetic words as, unlike some of the other towns where the professional team folded around the turn of the century, the amateur game remained in Ulverston and continues to this day.

The onset of professionalism was a disaster for a club such as Ulverston. Geographically isolated, it simply could not compete with the bigger town or city clubs which had a greater support, more financial resources and the ability to attract the better players. The costs of travelling and the unwillingness of the authorities to lend any financial support meant that, far from heralding a bright new dawn, the Northern Union very nearly signalled the death-knell for a club which in the mid 1890's appeared on the verge of establishing itself as a considerable force.

Walkden

FOUNDED: 1878
CEASED: 1899
REASON: financial difficulties
GROUND: Stocks Field
HEADQUARTERS: Stocks Hotel
COLOURS: Chocolate and blue

FROM its foundation Walkden played on a field, behind the Stocks Hotel, in the centre of the colliery village and acquired the nickname of the *Stocksmen*. In 1884 Walkden joined the Lancashire County Rugby Union and was one of the first clubs to put forward the idea of a cup or league competition to add interest to the fixture list and increase crowd support.

From the outset Walkden faced a great deal of competition for gate money. Association football was rapidly growing in popularity, especially in Lancashire around this time, with Walkden's near neighbour Bolton Wanderers a great rival. A couple of miles the other way down the road Swinton was establishing itself as one of the country's leading rugby organisations.

Admitted into membership of the West Lancashire Union in the 1887-88 season, Walkden competed in a cup competition for the first time. A defeat at the hands of Litherland denied Walkden a tie against Wigan. However, there was compensation for the *Stocksmen* when they entered, and won, the end-of-season Worsley Charity Cup competition.

Walkden staged the biggest game in its history when it hosted the Maoris on Wednesday 16 March 1889. It was the Maoris' 66th match of their mammoth tour but there was no reduction in interest. A crowd of 3500 turned up for the late afternoon kick-off and the event was a great success with the Walkden club easily covering the gate guarantee. Moreover, as the game attracted national attention it put Walkden firmly on the map, even though the tourists ran out convincing winners by one goal and three tries to one try and two minors.

The West Lancashire Cup ties were also a great appeal and Walkden reached the semi-final of the competition, before losing narrowly to Wigan in a game played at Leigh. The cup ties had been such a success that the senior clubs in the West Lancashire Union decided to form a league competition the following season. Eight clubs, Warrington, Aspull, Wigan, Leigh, Tyldesley, Widnes, St Helens and Walkden were included.

Wigan ran away with the league winning 13 of its 14 games, but Walkden was the only side to escape defeat at Wigan's hands, drawing at the Stocks Field in March and losing the return only narrowly a week later. Walkden finished second in the table and, with some shrewd player recruitment, began to build the strongest side in its own history.

The *Stocksmen* had nearly always relied on local talent but hereabouts a number of new players strengthened a predominantly forward-based side. The north Lancashire town of Askam was the source. Half-back Teddy Alexander, three-quarters Tom Vickers and Joe Pope and forwards Alf Duke and John Vickers were the first of a number of recruits.

The newcomers integrated into the team and forged a bond which served Walkden well throughout a challenging campaign. The players worked and played together, 15 of the 17 regular first-team members being directly employed in local collieries, the other two following trades as a shoe-maker and a carpenter.

Walkden enjoyed its finest season in 1890-91 when the West Lancashire League title was carried off. The *Stocksmen* knew that the

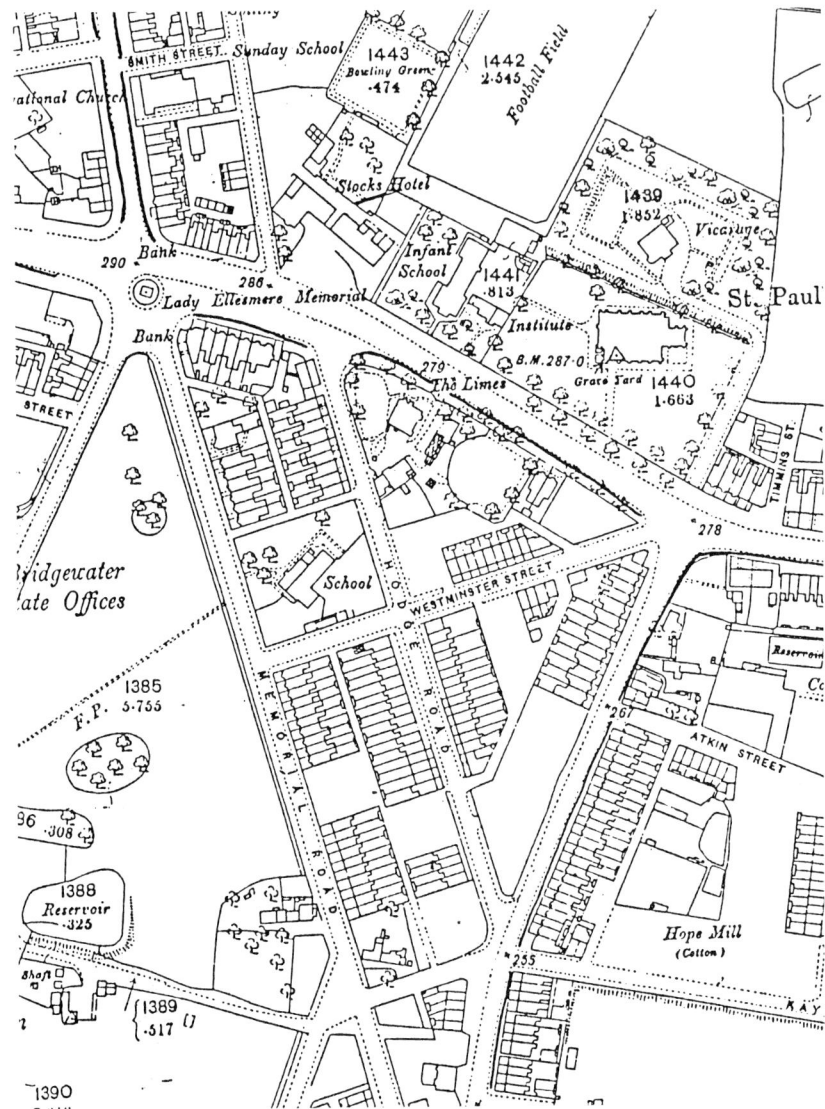

The Walkden club ground was situated behind Stocks Hotel, which was the club's headquarters and gave the club one of its nicknames, '"The Stocksmen". (Reproduced from 1893 Ordnance Survey Map)

two games against Wigan, scheduled for February, would in all likelihood decide the championship. Walkden pulled off a tremendous win on its visit to the Frog Lane enclosure and, in the return game a week later, again vanquished Wigan by two tries (both scored by Jimmy Martinscroft) to one. The village of Walkden was described as being "en fete" as the majority of a crowd, estimated at 6000, celebrated a notable double success. Walkden's championship was confirmed with a resounding home victory over St Helens, Tom Vickers scoring four of his side's seven tries.

Circumstances conspired to ensure that this was to be Walkden's finest hour. Some of the bigger clubs in the county wanted to free themselves from the constraints of league fixtures, which took up a dozen Saturdays during the season, usually when the weather was at its best. They wanted to play the best clubs from Yorkshire and other areas, as well as clubs such as Swinton, which was not in the league structure.

The lack of league games, however, resulted in a downturn of interest in the game. Clearly this situation could not be allowed to continue especially as the association code was continuing to make rapid strides so the Lancashire county committee formed a First Class competition in 1892 which soon saw interest revived, for the top clubs at least.

In 1893-94 Walkden became a founder member of the Second Class Competition finishing seventh out of ten clubs and sixth the following season. Forward Tom Whittaker became the first Walkden player to win county honours when he played against Glamorgan and Devon.

As the events of the summer of 1895 unfolded Walkden remained loyal to the Lancashire Rugby Union but then again had little choice in the matter. The club had simply not been invited to any of the clandestine meetings and hence was never in the reckoning to join the Northern Union. Major neighbouring clubs left the Rugby Union and Walkden was one of the clubs who filled the gaps, joining the ranks of the Lancashire Senior Competition for the 1895-96 season.

The major games were against Salford and Swinton but clubs from north of the county joined, adding considerably to Walkden's travelling expenses, with little compensation by way of gate receipts. After a poor start Walkden strung together some consistent form and finished eighth out of the eleven clubs which finished the season.

Walkden photographed c. 1895 (Photograph courtesy Mrs C E Mullineux)

With other clubs deciding to switch codes Walkden went with the flow and, before the campaign was out, journeyed to renew acquaintance with its old rivals Tyldesley. A 4-14 defeat at Well Street signalled Walkden's entry into the Northern Union.

The 1896-97 season saw Walkden, along with many other clubs, in limbo. Not having been invited into the inner sanctum of the leading Northern Union clubs, which had formed a 14-club Lancashire Senior Competition, and included new converts Swinton and Salford Walkden played a long string of friendly games against clubs in a similar position, fitting in some games against the top sides when there was a free date.

To spectators used to a regular diet of competitive league games the new situation was most unsatisfactory. Walkden's prospects deteriorated when Bolton Wanderers moved to a new ground at Burnden Park. This was generally considered to be a far superior enclosure than the previous one at Pikes Lane which was rather barren and not conducive to spectator comforts.

Results on the field were poor with many home attendances now numbered in only a few hundred and the club's financial state was a growing matter for concern. There was some consolation, however, from a trip to Hull in the Challenge Cup. Walkden lost 0-9 but the share of the gate money kept the club afloat.

Walkden was one of twelve clubs which formed a Lancashire Second Competition, in readiness for the 1897-98 season in an attempt to bring back some much-needed rivalry to fixtures. With the veterans Tom Vickers and Martinscroft still playing with considerable skill and the signing of a number of new players, including the Tyldesley pair of Billy Berry and Jimmy Tinker, there was a good deal of optimism that Walkden could turn the corner and restore some pride.

Walkden began the season with home wins over Altrincham and Crompton and it was noticeable that crowds were considerably up on the previous season. When Walkden played at nearby rival, Radcliffe an attendance of 3000 was registered at Peel Park.

The growing disparity in standards between senior and second-class clubs was demonstrated when Walkden lost heavily in a friendly to Swinton conceding nine tries. Walkden did put up a more creditable performance in the return engagement. "The Lions still think it polite enough to maintain the yearly engagements and thus display a practical interest in their less fortunate neighbours" reported the *Farnworth and Worsley Journal*.

Overall, Walkden performed with more distinction than might have been hoped at the start of the campaign by winning six and drawing four of its 18 league games. There was little to be gained in the long term, however, by being rated as "second-class" as spectators' interests and the attention of the local and national press was naturally focused on the senior clubs.

The geographical spread of the competing clubs also did little to help Walkden's increasingly parlous financial state. The only local clubs were Radcliffe and Barton and Walkden faced many long and expensive trips.

The Challenge Cup brought with it hope of some financial salvation and Walkden accepted a £40 guarantee from holders Batley to switch its home tie to Mount Pleasant much to the dismay of the club's loyal following. The game was a rather tame affair, with Walkden restricting Batley's attacking ideas but rarely threatening itself and the home side won 8-0.

It was generally felt that unless something was done then the following season would be the last in Walkden's history. A number of new players were brought in but they were largely junior signings or cast-offs from other clubs.

Walkden suffered from a serious lack of scoring power, being "nilled" in its opening three league games, and the traditional early season games against Swinton were providing financial consolation only. A 15-0 home win over competition newcomer and fellow struggler Blackpool brought Walkden its first two points of the season with Spencer scoring three tries in a fine individual performance but fortunes soon declined again.

By the turn of the year, however, Walkden's appearances on the football field were becoming infrequent. It had been noticeable that for a number of away games Walkden had been short-handed with players failing to turn up at the last minute. A lack of funds for broken-time was hardly an encouragement for players in an already struggling side.

Walkden gave evidence of its existence by playing Fleetwood in a home game on 21 January 1899 but the occasion was hardly cause for celebration. "The interest in the doings of the Walkden club has reached vanishing point" concluded the local newspaper. "The gates have steadily decreased for a long time and there was a mere handful of spectators present." Five substitutes were required at short notice to take the place of selected players who failed to turn up and a monotonous game ended in a 10-3 win for Fleetwood. Peter Vickers, younger brother of Tom, scored what proved to be Walkden's last try in Northern Union football.

A home fixture with Radcliffe on Saturday 18 February 1899 proved to be Walkden's last. The visitors dominated, running up 32 points without reply, in a game remarkably free of the rivalry which had marked many of the sides' previous meetings. Walkden's players looked dispirited from the start and Radcliffe scored seven tries the last of which was a length-of-the-field effort by Smith.

Radcliffe, which laboured under the same handicap as Walkden of having a successful Football League side on its doorstep, in this case Bury, struggled on until 1902 but for Walkden

Peter Vickers scored Walkden's last try in Northern Union football. He later played with some distinction for Wigan. (Photograph courtesy Nigel Winnard)

this was to be the final nail in the coffin.

After fulfilling 12 league games, significantly not making the long and costly trips to Barrow, Ulverston and Millom, Walkden threw in the towel. The club had limped along for some time and, in common with the apathy about its affairs, the end came with a whimper not a bang. At the monthly meeting of the Lancashire Second Competition at Preston, on 20 February 1899, the motion was given that Walkden be struck out of the competition for the non-fulfilment of fixtures.

Werneth

FOUNDED: c1880
CEASED: 1904
REASON: Changed name to Chadderton
GROUND: Block Lane
HEADQUARTERS: Hare and Hounds, Block Lane
COLOURS: Navy blue

WERNETH was regarded as a force in local rugby circles long before its elevation into the ranks of the Second Competition clubs in 1899. Progress would always be limited, however, by the close proximity of the Oldham club, at the time one of the most successful and wealthy in the game.

There existed a good relationship between the two clubs and Oldham's A team was regular visitors to Werneth's Block Lane enclosure, frequently attracting the junior club's best gate of the season. A good number of Oldham's players either started or finished their careers with the Werneth club.

Werneth was elected to membership of the Lancashire Rugby Union as early as March 1882. The other member clubs at this time were Liverpool, Walton, Swinton, Rochdale Hornets, Broughton, Broughton Rangers, Manchester Rangers, Cheetham, Cheetham Hill, Oldham, Manchester Free Wanderers and Widnes.

Founder members of the Rugby Union Lancashire Club Championship (Third Class) in 1893, Werneth finished in third position, behind Blackley Rangers and Pendleton. The following season Werneth slipped to sixth.

In 1895-96 Werneth found itself in the Second Class Competition due to the large number of withdrawals to join the Northern Union and, in the last campaign under the auspices of the Rugby Union, finished sixth. Werneth resigned from the Rugby Union in June 1896.

In terms of crowd support Werneth had more potential than many of the clubs invited to form the Second Competition, yet had to be content with being inaugural members of the Third Competition in 1897. Werneth proceeded to win the championship in its only season despite dropping three league points to its closest rival Whitworth.

The following season, 1898-99, Werneth played many of the Second Competition clubs in the South East Lancashire League and gave a good account of itself so, by the time it was elevated in status in 1899, the club expected to do well. A 0-31 defeat at Salford in the Challenge Cup, however, guarded against over-confidence.

Werneth's first match in the Lancashire Second Competition was on 2 September 1899, when the spoils were shared in a 6-6 draw at Fleetwood. A 0-3 defeat at Whitworth followed before Werneth made people sit up and take notice with a 3-2 win at newly-relegated Morecambe. Werneth now set the competition alight unearthing a rich vein of form, with ten successive wins, including a 10-8 success over championship favourites Barrow.

This game attracted a crowd of around 4000 to Block Lane, described in the *Barrow News*, with more than a whiff of bitterness, as "an apology of a ground." Surrounded by textile mills which made Oldham known as the "town of chimneys" the ground undoubtedly lacked spectator comforts and regularly attracted adverse comments.

Werneth had assembled a strong side with a number of former Oldham players, including former county centre Ike Taylor and forwards Bob Wyllie and Jim Moffatt. Sam Lees junior and Fred Daltry formed as good a half-back partnership as any in the league and, encouraged by the good gates, the Werneth committee secured the services of GH Lorriman, a talented three-quarter from Hudders-

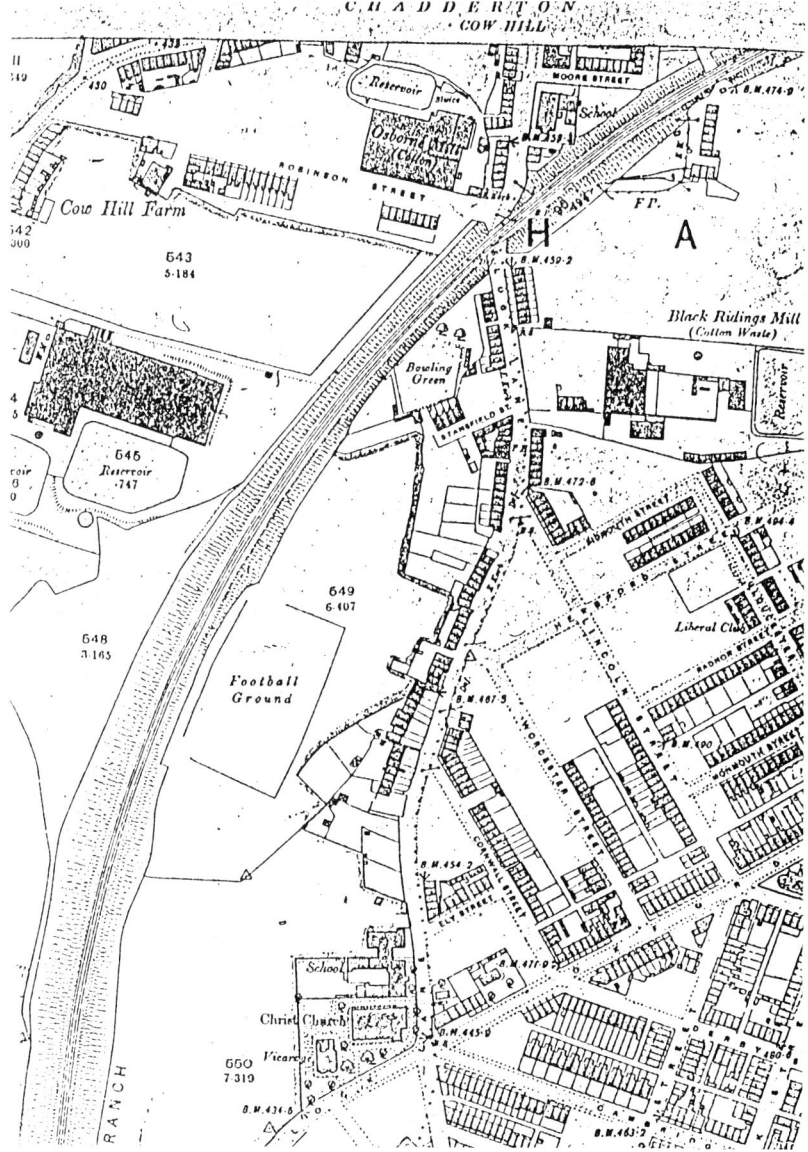

Werneth's ground was situated off Block Lane. (Reproduced from 1893 Ordnance Survey Map)

field. Squire Wormald, a goal-kicking centre, was also considered a fine acquisition.

Werneth also competed in the newly-formed Border Towns League but this competition, which Werneth won by virtue of victory over Rochdale Rangers in the final match, was disbanded after only one season due to a lack of funds. An appeal to the Lancashire and Yorkshire committees for financial assistance fell on deaf ears,

Werneth had high hopes of achieving senior status but fortunes declined after a 0-8 defeat at Barrow on New Year's Day. This proved to be a crucial game as Barrow went from strength to strength and won the league convincingly.

When Lancaster visited Block Lane in February, the crowd was down to a few hundred, a far cry from the regular £50 and £60 gates which had produced so much encouragement for Werneth's committee earlier in the campaign. Expectations had been raised only to be dashed but, even so, a final placing of second was highly satisfactory. Werneth won 14 and drew 3 of its 20 games finishing five points behind Barrow but five in front of third-placed Morecambe.

The following season it was noticeable that many of the "name" players who had appeared in the Werneth ranks were missing. The money had simply run out. The Werneth committee had to rely on local players with one or two exceptions, including the former Castleford half-back P Brady.

An early season win against eventual "champions" Morecambe raised hopes of a successful campaign but Werneth won only three of its first eleven league games, before finishing the season with a flourish, with five wins in the last six games.

There was an incredible mix-up on 6 October 1900 when Whitworth, according to Werneth's fixture card was due at Block Lane. A crowd of around 1500 were present, keenly anticipating the local "derby". Whitworth failed to turn up for the simple reason that it was at Tong Lane, together with a few hundred supporters, awaiting Werneth's arrival. Whitworth's fixture card, supplied by the Northern Union, also gave a home date. When the error was realised and the respective secretaries wired each other it was too late to make travelling arrangements and the fixture had to be rearranged.

For most games, however, crowds now numbered only a few hundred and the "floating" supporters, attracted by the prospect of success, disappeared quickly. Oldham, anxious to help its neighbour, granted £15 to Werneth to help ease the financial problems.

Werneth had been drawn to play at Workington in the Challenge Cup but decided to scratch from the competition. "It would cost £30 to get there and there was no guarantee of success" explained the *Oldham Chronicle*.

Werneth caused confusion when the team visited Ulverston, arriving in white jerseys instead of their usual blue. As the home side were similarly attired the Werneth players tied red ribbons round their arms so that the two sides could be distinguished.

Werneth's final game in the Lancashire Second Competition was on Easter Monday 8 April 1901. Birkenhead Wanderers came to Block Lane needing to win to lift the championship but Werneth's win, courtesy of a single penalty goal from the boot of full-back Turner Wood, meant that Morecambe became "champions" instead.

Werneth resumed life as a junior club after this season and became members of the Lancashire Combination, competing against the A teams of the county's senior clubs.

At the AGM of the Northern Union, held on 26 July 1904, Werneth was given permission to change its name to Chadderton, the colours to maroon and sky blue and the headquarters to the Cemetery Inn, Middleton Road. The club went on to finish third in the league behind Warrington A and Wigan A with 14 wins and a draw from 22 games.

After the 1905-06 season, despite again finishing third, Chadderton ceased to be a member of the Lancashire Combination and disappeared from the scene.

Whitworth

FOUNDED: early 1880's
CEASED: 1901
REASON: financial problems
GROUND: Tong Lane
HEADQUARTERS: at ground
COLOURS: Navy blue jerseys, white shorts

SITUATED three miles north of Rochdale, Whitworth was regarded as a junior club which was well respected in its locality. The fixture list comprised largely local engagements but on occasions, such as when Whitworth won the Rochdale Charity Cup in 1890, the club's deeds attracted attention. Known as "the Brown Backs" or "the Valley Men", Whitworth played at the Tong Lane ground in the centre of the town. Previously, the club had played at a ground described as "Bridge Mills." Whitworth first appeared in the Lancashire Club Championship in the 1895-96 season when the Lancashire Rugby Union committee invited the club to compete in the Second Class Competition. Whitworth had filled one of the places left by the clubs which left to join the Northern Union.

Despite a poor season, finishing seventh out of nine clubs, Whitworth found itself in the First Class Competition in 1896-97 again due to more clubs leaving the Rugby Union ranks.

Whitworth's decision to join the Northern Union came after the club had suffered two defeats at the hands of local rival, Castleton Moor, in the space of a fortnight. On 6 March 1897 Whitworth was knocked out of the Lancashire Cup at the first round stage and then lost in the Rochdale Charity Cup. Many of the clubs in Whitworth's league had departed to join the Northern Union and would have been left with a very small number of fixture opportunities had it remained in the Rugby Union.

Before the season was over Whitworth played three games under Northern Union rules and won them all. Whitworth beat Blackley Rangers 8-6 in its opening fixture on 3 April 1897 and then recorded victories over Rochdale Athletic and Radcliffe. In the summer of 1897 Whitworth became a founder member of the Lancashire Third Competition.

Highly confident of winning the championship at the beginning of the season, Whitworth began life in the new league with a 5-5 draw against Werneth. Whitworth won the return but was pipped for honours by its close rival.

Whitworth beat Boothstown and Todmorden twice each and Mossley, Rochdale Rangers, Warrington St Mary's and Leigh Shamrocks once in league games, losing against Rochdale Rangers, Warrington St Mary's and Leigh Shamrocks. The withdrawal during the season of Boothstown and Mossley cost Whitworth six points while another two were forfeited due to fielding an ineligible player.

Whitworth made its debut in the Challenge Cup, beating Rochdale Athletic after a replay, before going down 7-14 at Castleford. Whitworth "came close to effecting a great surprise" after a brave display. Whitworth's side was: Holt; Grindrod, Taylor, Heap, Fawthrop; Law, Heseltine; S Farmer, F Farmer, Hardman, Howarth, Kershaw, Malone, A Seddon, J Seddon. Taylor scored the try, Grindrod kicked two goals.

The Rochdale Charity Cup, a popular end-of-season competition, was played for the first time under Northern Union rules. With wins against Rochdale Athletic, Smallbridge, Littleborough and Rochdale Hornets A team, Whitworth brought the cup home scoring fifty points without reply during the competition. The final, played at Hornets' Dane Street ground on Saturday 2 April 1898, at-

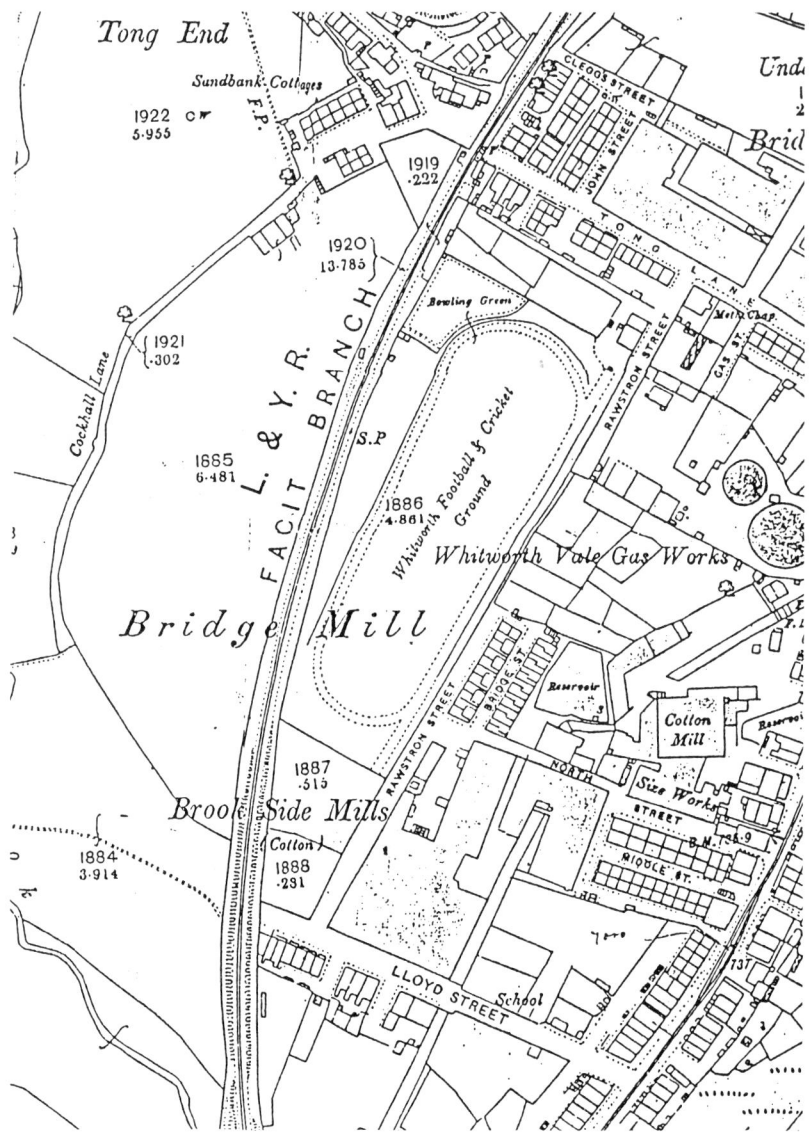

The Whitworth ground was situated off Tong Lane. (Reproduced from 1893 Ordnance Survey Map)

Whitworth

Whitworth following its victory in the Rochdale Charity Cup Final, 1890.
Back row: R Whitworth, W Brierley, S Taylor, J Alletson, W Greenwood, W H Howarth, H Law, J Stansfield, W Baynham, J Hill. **Middle row:** F J Smith, J Mills, F Crossley, E Norris, J Hough. **Front row:** G E Ashworth, E Chadwick, J Howarth.
(Photograph courtesy Whitworth Museum)

tracted a large crowd, Whitworth winning by a Taylor drop-goal in extra-time after the game had been scoreless.

Friendly games were also played against Barton, Fleetwood, Altrincham, Stockport A, Rochdale Rangers and Widnes A but, despite the varied fixture list and the interest generated by the league programme, gates "showed a great falling-off." The *Rochdale Observer* concluded that the club "need a great improvement in this direction to keep going."

The 1898-99 season was to prove a disappointing one as Whitworth was forced to play a series of friendly games due to the disbandment of the Third Competition. The only competitive fixtures were in the South East Lancashire League and the Challenge Cup. Whitworth met with little success in the league and lost to St Helens in the Cup. Despite a "fine tackling display" Whitworth was vanquished 3-12 by first division Saints. The *Valley Men's* hold on the Charity Cup was ended by a decisive 0-15 defeat at the hands of Hornets' A team.

Although the performances had been satisfactory Whitworth's financial state was described as poor and so promotion to the Lancashire Second Competition, due to the gaps left by the closure of Walkden and Barton, was looked upon with great enthusiasm.

Whitworth lost 0-5 to Morecambe in its first game under the Second Competition auspices. *The Morecambe Visitor*, in its match preview, was hardly complimentary towards the new opponent. "Whitworth have never heralded themselves as cracks in the football world" the report stated.

A 3-0 win over rival Werneth, courtesy of a try by Kershaw, was a signal that Whitworth would be a hard side to beat at home and only eventual "champions" Barrow won in the league at Tong Lane. Whitworth performed creditably, though the team's home form was in direct contrast to that shown on its travels, which included long and costly trips to Dalton, Barrow and Ulverston.

The financial situation was becoming serious with travelling expenses and players' wages outweighing money through the gate and hopes of a lucrative cup run were dashed by a 0-13 defeat at Radcliffe. For the home game against Ulverston, as a benefit to the club, players gave their services without reward and members paid for admittance.

Whitworth also played in the newly-formed Border Towns League, eventually won by Werneth, but many of the games attracted sparse crowds and the league closed down after only one season due to financial problems. The season did end on a high note, however, as Whitworth again won the Charity Cup. A crowd of 5000 at Dane Street witnessed a 5-0 success against Rochdale Rangers. Winger Brierley scored the game's only try and Grindrod dropped a goal and there were scenes of celebration as captain Kershaw lifted the cup.

The Lancashire Second Competition limped into a fourth season of operation in 1900-01 and, with only nine member clubs following Fleetwood's demise, there was an inevitable dearth of fixtures. Whitworth acquitted itself well in most of the fixtures and the *Birkenhead News* considered the team to be "the best-trained outfit in the competition." On the other hand the state of the Tong Lane ground often attracted criticism. "It is more like a quagmire than a field" reported the *Leigh Journal* after Tyldesley's visit.

The club was again not well supported and members were asked to pay for some games. It was hard to maintain interest as all but two of the league games had been completed by the end of January, especially after Whitworth lost 0-6 to Hebden Bridge in the Challenge Cup. The final home game of the season against Lancaster was a desultory affair, the visitors arriving with only ten men, while Whitworth had to scratch around for replacements to fill the gaps left by the absence of seven regulars. Whitworth, with a Towers try and Schofield goal eventually won 5-3.

The season was concluded with another appearance in the Charity Cup Final, Whitworth losing 0-5 to the Hornets A team at the Athletic Ground on Good Friday, 5 April 1901. There was some consolation in the share of a £57 gate.

This was to be Whitworth's final game. The growing financial strain could no longer be tolerated by the committee and, with support from the locals disappointing, Whitworth joined the ever-lengthening list of clubs to disband within a few years of joining the Northern Union bandwagon. The announcement, in the *Rochdale Observer* of 26 June 1901, was brief "The Whitworth club have given up the Rugby or Association code. Joe Taylor has signed for Leigh.....they evidently must need a three-quarter."

Whitworth's financial plight was nothing compared to that of Rochdale Hornets which, it was reported, had lost £702 on the season. The club was saved from going to the wall only by a successful Christmas bazaar which had raised over £1000. "The following season (1901-02) will be a trying one for all concerned" concluded the *Rochdale Observer*. "Clubs simply cannot continue with the same expenses as before."

LANCASHIRE SECOND COMPETITION 1897-98

	P	W	D	L	F	A	Pts
Barrow	18	13	1	4	237	59	27
Millom	18	13	1	4	173	55	27
Ulverston	18	10	2	6	101	75	22
Radcliffe	18	9	2	7	107	117	20
Lancaster	18	9	1	8	94	96	19
Barton	18	8	2	8	107	114	18
Birkenhead Wanderers	18	7	2	9	118	94	16
Walkden	18	6	4	8	79	143	16
Altrincham	18	6	1	11	54	95	13
Fleetwood	18	1	0	17	41	263	2

Crompton and St. Helens Recs disbanded during the season and their results were expunged from the table

LANCASHIRE SECOND COMPETITION 1898-99

	P	W	D	L	F	A	Pts
Millom	16	15	1	0	301	15	31
Barrow	16	10	3	3	190	41	23
Lancaster	16	9	1	6	121	77	19
Ulverston	15	8	2	5	68	52	18
Altrincham	15	6	4	5	85	48	16
Radcliffe	16	7	1	8	119	69	15
Birkenhead Wanderers	16	7	1	8	101	126	15
Fleetwood	16	2	1	13	48	221	5
Blackpool	16	0	0	16	31	415	0

Barton and Walkden disbanded during the season and their results were expunged from the table

LANCASHIRE SECOND COMPETITION 1899-1900

	P	W	D	L	F	A	Pts
Barrow	20	17	2	1	254	34	36
Werneth	20	14	3	3	135	64	31
Morecambe	20	11	4	5	147	52	26
Birkenhead Wanderers	19	9	2	8	80	103	20
Whitworth	20	9	1	10	102	146	19
Altrincham	19	8	1	10	90	106	17
Lancaster	20	6	3	11	114	108	15
Fleetwood	19	6	3	10	48	110	15
Radcliffe	18	6	1	11	75	105	13
Ulverston	19	5	1	13	43	160	11
Dalton	16	3	1	12	38	138	7

LANCASHIRE SECOND COMPETITION 1900-01

	P	W	D	L	F	A	Pts
Morecambe	16	12	0	4	107	53	24
Birkenhead Wanderers	16	11	0	5	111	37	22
Lancaster	16	8	2	6	94	58	18
Altrincham	16	8	1	7	108	64	17
Radcliffe	16	8	1	7	72	95	17
Werneth	16	7	1	8	66	72	15
Whitworth	16	7	0	9	55	78	14
Tyldesley	16	6	1	9	59	89	13
Leigh Shamrocks	16	2	0	14	33	159	4

Fleetwood disbanded during the season and its results were expunged from the table

SUBSCRIBERS

R BRYAN SMITH, FCA
ANTHONY HOLSTEAD, Harrogate
D BUTTERFIELD
D E ELSE
S P HADDEN
J MELIA
G MORRIS
ANDREW HARDCASTLE, Halifax
ADRIAN McGUIRE
STEVE LAWRENCE - Secretary of British RL Referees Association
JOE THORNTON
PAUL HOUGH
TONY ACKROYD (Halifax & Keighley)
BOB EVANS
GARY PORTER
GARY AUSTIN
MALCOLM FERGUSON
MARTIN GLEESON
BERNARD ROWLIN, RL Supporter
ERNIE DAY
DAVID CRAVEN, Illingworth, Halifax
CHRIS, LYNNE & NATALIE (Wigan RLFC)
BRIAN LEATHER
ROWENA AND EDMUND TONGE - love from dad
ALAN J MARK

ESB MOTOR CYCLES (Leigh & Bolton)

GRAHAM WILLIAMS
RON BROWN, Leeds
PETER A MOIR
MICHAEL JACKSON (Cas fan)
J C PETRIE
ROGER GRIME
J NIGEL WINNARD
MR B WHITE
R H PANTON
MICHAEL INMAN
ALEX SERVICE (St Helens)
ALAN WATERHOUSE
RUGBY FOOTBALL LEAGUE, ARCHIVES
STUART BERRY
DONALD DOCKER
E PHILIP HARRISON (Yorkshire County Rugby League)
GEOFFREY MOORHOUSE
C KINGHAM
T J HALL
JOHN DOTTERS
TERRY CASEY
JOHN S EDWARDS

BILL LYTHGOE
DAVE HADFIELD (The Independent)
R B AUSTIN, Knaresborough
MARGARET RATCLIFFE
A D HANSON
STEPHEN BOOTHROYD
JOHN EVANS
DAVID W MARSH
G JUMPS
S EVANS, York RL Historian
L BURGESS
ALLAN ROGERSON
BILL NELSON
BARROW LIBRARY
M A TAYLOR
OLDHAM LOCAL STUDIES LIBRARY
BILL RILEY
FARNWORTH LIBARY
PETER WILLIAM OSBALDISTON
DANIEL MINKIN
PETER RHODES
JOE HOLLIDAY, Workington
IN MEMORY OF TOM AND LILY RIGBY
MRS N MOORE, Nelson, Lancs

SPORTSPAGES, The Specialist Sports Bookshop, 94-96 Charing Cross Road, London and Barton Square, St Annes Square, Manchester

BURY LIBRARY
TONY POCOCK
RAY GARDNER, Barrow-In-Furness
DON RAINGER
RUGBY LEAGUE SUPPORTERS ASSOCIATION
DICK GILLINGHAM, Blackpool RL Supporters
R & S GORRIE
A P MAITLAND, St Annes
M CRANE, Thornton-Cleveleys
DR R M BROADLEY, Thornton-Cleveleys
D COCKCROFT, Blackpool
TOM & "TERRY" WILLIAMS, Thornton
IAN JACKSON, Swinton RLFC
IAN M WILLIAMS
JOHN H BARKER
J M WHITE
IAN WARD
TREVOR DELANEY
C WARBURTON
JOHN B GRIFFIN
RODNEY SYKES
BLACKWELL'S ACADEMIC BOOKSHOP, Manchester

SUBSCRIBERS (continued)

R RYAN
DAVID C MAKIN
STEVE SKEAVINGTON (Nottingham City RIP)
G BOLTON, RL supporter for 41 years
CHRIS M J WILSON
JOHN GILL
KARL SPRACKLEN
JIM BRENNAN (Wigan and Workington Town)
FRANCIS TAYLOR
HARVEY DAVIS
ST HELENS MBC
T O'COIRBIN, Liverpool
DARRELL PLATT
MORLEY BOOK CO LTD, Morley, Leeds
JOHN WILLIAMS
C HEWISON
DUNCAN S MERCER
GEOFF APPLETON
LOUIS BONNERY, Limoux, France
LEIGH LIBRARY
IAN JOHNSON
JIM SAVAGE
TERRY BRENNEN

GED HAYES
CHRIS HARTE
ROBIN ISHERWOOD

CHAMLEYS (BOOKSELLERS & STATIONERS), Union Street, Leigh

J COBB
C DILLEY
S ALI
DEREK LATHAM
MONA LATHAM
JENNIFER LATHAM
SARAH LATHAM
JANET LATHAM

SMITHS OF WIGAN, 41 Mesnes St. Wigan. Tel: (0942) 42810

OSCAR AND JASPER
ASKEWS LIBRARY BOOK SUPPLY, Preston
WIGAN MBC, LIBRARIES SECTION

THE DINGLE HOTEL, Rectory Lane, Lymm, Cheshire. Tel: (0925) 752297

PREVIOUS TITLES FROM MIKE RL PUBLICATIONS

LEIGH RLFC - AN ILLUSTRATED HISTORY
by Michael Latham and Mike Hulme
76 pages Published 1990 Price £ 4.95
ISBN 0 9516098 0 7

The story of one of Rugby League's founder members, extensively illustrated and including a hall of fame and records section.

THEY PLAYED FOR LEIGH
by Michael Latham
52 pages Published 1991 Price £ 4.95
ISBN 0 9516098 1 5

A statistical and pictorial study of the Leigh club's players' records and achievements (1895-1991) containing many rare and interesting photographs.

THEY PLAYED FOR WIGAN
by Michael Latham and Robert Gate
76 pages Published 1992 Price £ 5.99
ISBN 0 9516098 2 3

A statistical record of every player to play for Wigan (1895-1992) together with individual club records and honours. Extensively illustrated with many rare photographs.

Coveropen Ltd.

BOOK PRODUCTION CONSULTANTS
MANUSCRIPT-TO-BOOK SERVICE

Specialist producers for self-publishing organisations, societies and individuals

UNBIASED FREE ADVICE TO ACCOMMODATE ALL BUDGETS

5 Bridgeman Terrace, Wigan WN1 1SX
Tel: (0942) 821831 • Fax: (0942) 821819